RACE, SLAVERY AND THE CIVIL WAR

RACE, SLAVERY
AND THE
CIVIL WAR

THE TOUGH STUFF OF
AMERICAN HISTORY AND MEMORY

Edited by James O. Horton *and* Amanda Kleintop

Virginia Sesquicentennial of the American Civil War Commission
Richmond, Virginia

ISBN 978-0-9834012-0-9

The second in a series of annual Signature Conferences sponsored by
the Virginia Sesquicentennial of the American Civil War Commission,
"Race, Slavery and the Civil War: The Tough Stuff of American History
and Memory" was held on September 24, 2010.

Library of Congress Control Number: 2011924372

Virginia Sesquicentennial of the American Civil War Commission
Richmond, Virginia

www.VirginiaCivilWar.org

CONTENTS

PANEL II: THE TOUGH STUFF OF AMERICAN HISTORY AND MEMORY

Acknowledgments

While it may not be possible to fully capture the spirit of a big moment in print, this book is offered in the hopes that it conveys to the reader the fullness of this daylong program: lively discussions, dynamic exchanges, thoughtful and reflective moments, and lighter moments and laughter—all in a spirit of warmth and welcome.

The success of this program is attributable to many people, and foremost is Conference Chair James O. Horton, for his vision and leadership. When we first approached Jim Horton about the idea of chairing a conference on race and slavery in the Civil War, he jumped at the chance. Much of Jim's scholarship has been dedicated to examining the relationship between slavery and the Civil War, and he immediately began to make a list of topics to cover and friends who might join the conversation. It is a benefit to us all that those friends include many of the top Civil War historians in the nation, and we are forever grateful for the illumination they brought to the conference: Ira Berlin, David Blight, Spencer Crew, Harold Holzer, Bruce Levine, James McPherson, Edna Greene Medford, Cassandra Newby-Alexander, Dwight T. Pitcaithley, and Jean Fagan Yellin.

Norfolk State University provided the perfect venue for this important program, and the faculty, staff, and students exhibited NSU's characteristic drive for excellence. We are especially grateful for the leadership of Kim Luckes, Acting President, and the conference host committee, led by Charles Ford, Cassandra Newby-Alexander, and Crystal Square-Williams.

Ensuring that the program ran smoothly were the Master of Ceremonies, the Honorable Algie T. Howell, Jr., and the Question Managers, William Alexander and Geoffrey deLaforcade. We appreciate the support of Maris Rence and Joyce Lee, who provided everything we needed at the beautiful Wilder Performing Arts Center. The full NSU community offered assistance at every turn, and dozens of students in Spartan gold shirts volunteered their time to welcome and guide the conference attendees and guests.

The Commission gratefully acknowledges the support of the Dominion Foundation, the Verizon Foundation, the History Channel, the Virginia Foundation for the Humanities, and donors in the Civil War 150 Council, whose generosity made the second Signature Conference possible.

The success of the conference series and of this book is due in large measure to the superb direction of Cheryl Jackson, the Commission's executive director, and to the tireless dedication of staff and volunteers. Shaping the proceedings of a daylong conference into a cohesive book is a considerable undertaking. The work was handled with great skill by Amanda Kleintop and Kathleen DuVall, with assistance from Dan Rudary. We are grateful for the care they have taken to ensure that this volume will endure for generations.

William J. Howell, Chairman
Virginia Sesquicentennial of the American Civil War Commission

Chronology of Emancipation

1860

NOVEMBER 6 Abraham Lincoln is elected president.

DECEMBER 20 South Carolina becomes the first southern state to secede from the Union.

1861

FEBRUARY 4 Convention of the first six seceded states, South Carolina, Mississippi, Florida, Alabama, Georgia, Louisiana, meets in Montgomery, Alabama, adopts provisional constitution of the Confederate States of America on February 8, and elects Jefferson Davis provisional president on February 9.

MARCH 2 U.S. Congress adopts and sends to the states a constitutional amendment (which fails of ratification) forbidding any subsequent amendment to "abolish or interfere . . . with the domestic institutions" of the states.

MARCH 4 President Lincoln is inaugurated.

APRIL 12 Civil War begins with Confederate attack on federal garrison at Fort Sumter, South Carolina.

APRIL 15 President Lincoln issues proclamation calling for troops to put down the rebellion.

APRIL 17 Virginia's State Secession Convention adopts the Ordinance of Secession.

MAY 24 Fugitive slaves at Fortress Monroe, Virginia, are received and put to work by Union general Benjamin F. Butler, who declares them "contraband of war."

JULY 21 Confederate victory at Battle of Bull Run (Manassas) dashes Union hopes of quelling the rebellion quickly and without great loss of life.

AUGUST 6 First Confiscation Act nullifies owners' claims to fugitive slaves who had been employed in the Confederate war effort.

AUGUST 30 Invoking martial law, General John C. Frémont declares free the slaves of disloyal owners in Missouri; President Lincoln asks that Frémont modify the order so as not to exceed congressional laws respecting emancipation.

1862

MARCH 13 U.S. Congress adopts an additional article of war forbidding members of the army and navy to return fugitive slaves to their owners.

APRIL 10 At Lincoln's request, Congress pledges financial aid to any state that undertakes gradual emancipation with compensation to owners.

APRIL 16 Congress abolishes slavery in the District of Columbia, with compensation to loyal owners, and appropriates money for the voluntary removal ("colonization") of former slaves to Haiti, Liberia, and other countries.

JUNE 19 Congress prohibits slavery in the territories.

JULY 17 Congress passes and Lincoln signs the Second Confiscation Act, which frees the slaves of persons engaged in or assisting the rebellion and provides for the seizure and sale of other property owned by disloyal citizens; it forbids army and navy personnel to decide on the validity of any fugitive slave's claim to freedom or to surrender any fugitive to any claimant, and authorizes the president to employ "persons of African descent" in any capacity to suppress the rebellion.

JULY 17 Militia Act, passed by Congress, provides for the employment of "persons of African descent" in "any military or naval service for which they may be found competent," granting freedom to slaves so employed (and to their families if they belong to disloyal owners).

JULY 22 President Lincoln announces to his cabinet his intention to issue a proclamation freeing slaves in the rebel states, but agrees to postpone it until after a suitable military victory.

SEPTEMBER 17 Confederate invasion of Maryland repulsed at Antietam.

SEPTEMBER 22 Preliminary Emancipation Proclamation is issued by President Lincoln; it announces that all slaves in those states or portions of states still in rebellion as of January 1, 1863 will be declared free; pledges monetary aid for slave states not in rebellion that adopt either immediate or gradual emancipation; and reiterates support for the colonization of freed slaves outside the U.S.

DECEMBER 23 Confederate President Jefferson Davis issues proclamation ordering that black Union soldiers and their officers captured by Confederate troops are not to be treated as prisoners of war; instead, they are to be remanded to Confederate state authorities.

1863

JANUARY 1 Emancipation Proclamation is issued by President Lincoln; it declares free all slaves in the Confederate states (except Tennessee, southern Louisiana, and parts of Virginia) and announces the Union's intention to enlist black soldiers and sailors. By late spring, recruitment is under way throughout the North and in all Union-occupied Confederate states except Tennessee.

MAY 22 Bureau of Colored Troops is created within the War Department.

JULY 30 President Lincoln pledges that Union soldiers, black or white, are entitled to equal protection if captured by the enemy and threatens retaliation for Confederate enslavement of black prisoners of war.

DECEMBER 8 President Lincoln issues a Proclamation of Amnesty and Reconstruction, offering pardon and restoration of property (except slaves) to Confederates who take an oath of allegiance to the Union and accept emancipation; it proposes a plan by which loyal voters of a seceded state can begin the process of readmission to the Union.

1864

APRIL 8 Senate approves constitutional amendment abolishing slavery.

JUNE 15 House of Representatives fails to approve constitutional amendment abolishing slavery. Congress makes pay of black soldiers (which had been $10 per month for all ranks) equal to that of white soldiers ($13 per month for privates, larger amounts for higher ranks); the change is retroactive to January 1, 1864, or, for men who were free before the war, to the time of enlistment.

OCTOBER 13 Maryland Constitution is ratified, emancipating slaves in Maryland.

NOVEMBER 8 Abraham Lincoln is re-elected president, defeating George B. McClellan.

1865

JANUARY 12 General William T. Sherman and Secretary of War Edwin M. Stanton meet with twenty black leaders in Savannah, Georgia, to discuss the future of the ex-slaves.

JANUARY 31 House of Representatives approves constitutional amendment abolishing slavery, sending it to the states for ratification.

MARCH 3 Congress approves joint resolution liberating the wives and children of black soldiers, and establishes Bureau of Refugees, Freedmen, and Abandoned Lands (Freedmen's Bureau) to oversee the transition from slavery to freedom.

MARCH 13 Confederate Congress authorizes President Jefferson Davis to recruit enslaved men as soldiers with the permission of their owners; Confederate War Department issues order governing the enlistment on March 23.

APRIL 9 Surrender of General Robert E. Lee and Army of Northern Virginia to Union Army under Lt. General Ulysses S. Grant occurs at Appomattox Court House, Virginia.

APRIL 14 President Lincoln is assassinated; Vice President Andrew Johnson succeeds to the presidency.

DECEMBER 18 Ratification of the Thirteenth Amendment to the U.S. Constitution is announced by the Secretary of State abolishing slavery throughout the U.S.

Based in part on Freedmen and Southern Society Project, *Chronology of Emancipation during the Civil War.* www.history.umd.edu/Freedmen/chronol.htm. Used with permission.

Race, Slavery and the Civil War

INTRODUCTION

JAMES O. HORTON

One hundred fifty years of history have passed since the American Civil War, years that were marked by the war and profoundly shaped by it. The Civil War is one of the most important conflicts in American history, and in some ways the most devastating and disruptive. In a nation with a population at that time of thirty million people, the Civil War cost more than six hundred thousand lives. Proportionally, such a war today would cost the United States more than six million lives. This comparison must stand in our consideration of the war and its legacies.

The Great Contradiction

The most significant legacy of the Civil War, arguably, was that it ended slavery as America's great contradiction. To understand the inherent contradiction of slavery, we first must return to the 1770s—the American colonists who clashed with Great Britain, pushing for liberty for the American people until they reached the point of war. The revolutionaries were fighting for a great contradiction, for a freedom that did not mean freedom for all.

During the time when Americans were considering the

possibility of freeing themselves from Britain, they talked about their predicament in ways that would seem to reject their own slaveholding society. Josiah Quincy, a lawyer, patriot, and spokesman for the Sons of Liberty in Boston, expressed his displeasure with America's subservience to Great Britain: "I speak it with shame, I speak it with indignation, we are slaves." Many Americans at the time agreed with this statement. As Pennsylvanian John Dickinson explained, "Those who are taxed without their own consent, as expressed by themselves or their representatives, are slaves." The American revolutionaries used rhetoric of enslavement under Great Britain to justify the Revolutionary War.

This argument became even more important as the colonists considered going to war against a nation that was, at the time, the strongest military power in the world. But the American patriots believed that God had provided human beings with the right to freedom, which included freedom from taxation without representation. When these rights were proclaimed by the American people, they were based on an assumption of equality. As Thomas Jefferson wrote in the Declaration of Independence, "We hold these truths to be self-evident, that all men are created equal, that they are endowed by their Creator with certain unalienable Rights, that among these are Life, Liberty and the pursuit of Happiness."

Herein lies a true contradiction: the man who wrote that God gave human beings the right to life, liberty, and the pursuit of happiness was, at the time he wrote those words on paper, holding a hundred and fifty people in slavery. This contradiction between what America stood for and what it practiced was a contradiction that many people at the time understood. The British recognized the inconsistency. British writer Samuel Johnson challenged the revolutionary rhetoric in March 1775, asking, "How is it that we hear the loudest yelps for liberty among the drivers of Negroes?"

Furthermore, in 1773, slaves in Massachusetts petitioned the legislature in Boston, echoing revolutionary language: "We expect great things from men who have determined not to allow themselves to be enslaved by fellow men." These people demanded inclusion in the struggle for liberty.

By the time the American Revolution was approaching, slavery had been in existence in the British North American colonies for one hundred fifty years. The first slaves came in 1619 to Jamestown, Virginia. Slavery's economic importance only grew as Americans moved into the Revolution and evolved from thirteen colonies into one nation. It is important to note that slavery at this time was not necessarily a strictly Southern institution. There were slaves all over the United States, in New York, Pennsylvania, various parts of New England, and elsewhere. But moving into the nineteenth century, northern states and territories began gradually and unevenly to abolish slavery.

The institution of slavery prompted many questions for the new nation, as some found it quite embarrassing. America's Founding Fathers attempted to satisfy both those whose livelihoods depended on slavery and others who seriously questioned the viability of slavery in a nation based on a belief in freedom. One of these compromises was built into the Constitution: The Three-Fifths Compromise allowed slave states to count three-fifths of their slaves toward their total population, giving them greater representation in the House of Representatives. This was just one of the compromises that sought to reconcile the arguments that were developing between slaveholders and non-slaveholders.

In the nineteenth century, the institution of slavery became more and more powerful. For example, production of cotton in the South was done, for the most part, by slave labor. Cotton was becoming more and more profitable, not only to the South, but to the entire nation. In 1793, Eli Whitney had invented a machine called the cotton gin, which helped workers remove seeds from cotton fiber, a task that was originally performed slowly by hand, one seed at a time. The cotton gin made this a more rapid process, allowing one slave to do as much work as fifty had done prior to its invention. By 1840, the value of cotton was greater than the value of any other American export. This increased the economic power of the slaveholding South as well as the economic and political importance of slavery.

Just before the Civil War, the value of all the slaves in the United States was greater than the value of all of America's banks, railroads, and manufacturing combined. Slavery was central to American society, and it provided great economic power to the slaveholders. Then, as now, economic power often translated into political power. There were seventy-two years between the election of George Washington and the election of Abraham Lincoln. For fifty of those years, slaveholders held the office of President of the United States. The power of slaveholders spread to much of the nation and, incidentally, to much of the world.

While the American South provided cotton to the northern textile industry, it was also providing that raw material to countries around the world, notably Great Britain. This further entrenched the institution of slavery, and it had great political ramifications. When the southern secessionists spoke of seceding from the Union, many believed they could expect international support from nations that depended upon their cotton. This was an important consideration when they were conceptualizing the establishment of an independent nation.

American Memory

Considering the economic and political weight of slavery as an American institution, it is important that we recognize that slavery was a major cause of the Civil War. This statement is nonetheless controversial. But when the social, political, and economic needs of the South are viewed through the eyes of southerners, slavery stood out in all aspects of southern society.

As we all know, the Civil War eventually brought slavery to an end. But the American memory of the war is complicated and ever-changing, and it tells us something about our society today. For example, many current racial assumptions, what we might call racial profiling, came from an effort that goes all the way back to just after the Revolution, arguments that were used to reconcile holding black people in slavery with the American ideal of freedom. African Americans were seen as incapable of dealing with freedom; rather, they were to be protected under a kind of paternalism. After slavery was over, racial theory was used to support segregation, and today we talk about racial profiling.

As the justifications for slavery and freedom show, our memory of the Civil War tells us a lot about our society before, during, and after the Civil War. I can recount personal experiences with people who want to deny that the Civil War was about slavery in any way. I gave a lecture about four years ago at Harpers Ferry, and many in the audience wore Civil War uniforms—mostly Confederate—only about two or three were wearing blue.

The title of my lecture was "Slavery and the Coming of the Civil War," and it was clear that most of the people in the audience would not believe that the Civil War had anything to do with slavery. I could not convince them alone, so my strategy was to quote as many Confederate leaders and heroes as possible, demonstrating through their words that the threat to slavery was why they were seceding.

I quoted one Confederate in particular, the leader of a number of opposition groups. His name was John Singleton Mosby, and he was called "The Gray Ghost." After the Civil War Mosby wrote, "South Carolina went to war—as she said in her Secession proclamation—because slavery would not be secure under Lincoln," then adding, "South Carolina ought to know what was the cause for her seceding." Mosby, a Confederate hero, understood that South Carolina, the first southern state to secede, seceded because of slavery.

Of course, this strategy of using the words of the Confederate leaders is not foolproof. A lot of what affects the American memory of the Civil War is a lack of information about the period. For example, secessionists in South Carolina pressed for secession with such urgency because they believed that if Abraham Lincoln became president he would free all of the slaves. While Lincoln was not in favor of slavery, he was not a radical abolitionist. He wanted to stop the spread of slavery into the new Western territories. In his first inaugural address, he stated, "I have no purpose, directly or indirectly, to interfere with the institution of slavery in the States where it exists." But many people did not believe Lincoln's words and assumed that as long as he was in office the institution of slavery—and therefore the whole southern economic system—would be in jeopardy.

There were those outside of the South who also assumed that Lincoln would free the slaves. During the presidential campaign in New York, Democrats predicted that if Lincoln freed the slaves, emancipated southern slaves would come to New York and compete with white New Yorkers for the advantages and jobs available there. Lincoln won the state of New York in the presidential race, but not by much, because many people took the Democrats' warnings seriously. Although he won the presidency, there were many people, even in the North, who were worried that Lincoln was an abolitionist.

In spite of all this, Lincoln is remembered as the Emancipator because of the Emancipation Proclamation. Part of the reason he issued the Proclamation is that it would appeal to anti-slavery people in other countries, such as Great Britain, who otherwise might very well support the Confederacy. The Proclamation did not apply to all places in the nation; it applied only to Confederate states that were at war against the Union (except Union-occupied Tennessee, southern Louisiana, and parts of Virginia).

A greater irony is seen in the Thirteenth Amendment, the constitutional amendment that abolished slavery in the United States after the Civil War. In the North, before the Civil War, slavery had been abolished gradually, for the most part. If a child was born to an enslaved mother before abolition laws went into effect, the child was enslaved. And if a child was born to an enslaved mother after the abolition laws went into effect, he or she had to reach a certain age to be free. That was true in New Jersey, New York, and several other states in the North, so there were still a few slaves in the North as the Civil War was approaching. After the Civil War, when the Thirteenth Amendment was ratified, it freed about sixteen slaves in New Jersey. Because slavery had not been fully abolished in the North, some people to this day reject southern slavery as a cause of the Civil War. But historical evidence points to the conflict over slavery as a major catalyst.

The records left behind can help us understand why the southern states seceded. The Secession Convention documents, for example, show us what kinds of arguments were being made in the state meetings where secession was debated. And it is at conferences like this one, where thoughtful and learned people gather, information is disseminated and interpreted, preconceived notions are challenged, and discussion is encouraged, that we gain a wider view of the Civil War and emancipation and a more nuanced understanding of the United States of America past and present.

OPENING REMARKS

ROBERT F. MCDONNELL
GOVERNOR OF VIRGINIA

Thank you, President Kim Luckes, Rector Ed Hamm, and the Norfolk State University community for hosting all of us today. I also want to thank the General Assembly, Cheryl Jackson, and the staff of the Sesquicentennial Commission for planning for years to take on these pivotal issues.

On behalf of the Commonwealth of Virginia, I welcome scholars and leaders from around the nation to this very important conference to discuss the truly tough stuff of the American Civil War. Virginia now begins the four-year period marking the 150th Anniversary of the Civil War. A prosperous, dynamic, and diverse Commonwealth is attempting to remember, understand, and put into proper perspective one of the most painful and bloody periods in the history of Western civilization. This is not going to be easy. I know that from firsthand experience.

In the century and a half since Lee's surrender at Appomattox, few states have undergone as many changes or witnessed such stunning growth and progress as our Commonwealth. Our borders have been fixed for 147 years, but our culture, community, and breadth of opportunity have been incredibly dynamic. These changes have made Virginia a stronger and better place. But they have also made our collective "memory"—how our diverse society remembers and processes the events in its collective history—much more complicated.

In earlier times, Virginia's dominant culture was defined by relatively few, and basic civil rights were excluded for many. Whatever the strengths and weaknesses of that culture—and both were present in abundance, as in any human enterprise—there was a common lens through which to view history. Those in power wrote a single, narrow narrative. It left out many people, along with their powerful stories.

And so, while talking about our history has become more complicated today, we can all agree it has also become a much richer conversation. Today we are a Commonwealth of eight million people, and one in ten citizens are foreign born. We come from many different countries, backgrounds, and traditions. Modern Virginia is a place of great natural beauty, hope, and opportunity, a place refined in the crucible of conflict, and renewed in its commitment to the founding ideal of equal liberty and justice and opportunity for all.

We have made progress together in Virginia. The nation's first African-American governor. An African American is Chief Justice of the Supreme Court. The nation's first official expression of "profound regret" for slavery from a legislature. A marvelous civil rights memorial in front of the Governor's Mansion, and a wonderful new portrait of Barbara Johns that I helped unveil in the State Capitol.

In my inaugural address, I tried to tell this story of progress and reflect on Virginia's common history. I stood on the steps of the State Capitol, looking down toward the James River, the waterway of the settlers. The building behind me was designed by Virginia's second governor, Thomas Jefferson. Inside it, Robert E. Lee, the son of a Virginia governor, took command of Virginia's military forces in 1861. Four years later, President Abraham Lincoln visited the Capitol as the fallen city around it burned. In 1990, that same building welcomed the inauguration of my friend, Governor Doug Wilder, the grandson of slaves. And now I stood there, a descendant of ancestors who were poor farmers in Ireland in the 1860s. An average middle-class kid from Fairfax County became part of that gubernatorial tradition tracing back to Patrick Henry.

I was far less successful in capturing the full meaning of our history when, four months later, I issued a proclamation concerning Confederate History Month. My major and unacceptable omission of slavery disappointed and hurt a lot of people, myself included. Young people make mistakes, and I suppose sometimes young administrations do as well. Ours was an error of haste and not of heart. And it is an error that will be fixed.

Next April our office will issue a "Civil War in Virginia" proclamation commemorating the beginning of the Civil War in our state. This proclamation will encapsulate all of our history. It will remember all Virginians, free and enslaved, Union and Confederate. It will be written for all Virginians. While we cannot fully put to paper the definitive collective memory of this period, we are going to at least ensure that all voices are heard in the attempt.

The legacies of the Civil War still have the potential to divide us. But there is a central lesson of that conflict that must bond us together today. Until the Civil War, the founding principle that all people are created equal and endowed by their Creator with unalienable rights was dishonored by slavery. Slavery was an evil and inhumane practice which degraded people to property, defied the eternal truth that all people are created in the image and likeness of God, and left a stain on the soul of this state and nation. For this to be truly one nation under God required the abolition of slavery from our soil. Until the Emancipation Proclamation was issued and the Civil War ended, our needed national reconciliation could not begin. It is still a work in progress. One hundred fifty years is long enough for Virginia to fight the Civil War.

Now, on the eve of this anniversary, is a time for us to approach this period with a renewed spirit of goodwill, reverently recalling its losses, eagerly embracing its lessons, and celebrating the measure of unity we have achieved as a diverse nation united by the powerful idea of human freedom. A modern Virginia has emerged from her past—strong, vibrant, and diverse. Now, a modern Virginia will remember that past with candor, courage, and conciliation.

It is my hope that the work of the Sesquicentennial Commission will bear much fruit, starting with this conference. Beginning in 2011, people will come from across the world to see the solemn battlefields of Virginia, home to more than any other state, and we encourage and welcome that tourism.

Experts will come to conferences and appear on TV and debate the causes, tactics, and legacy of the war that divided America, and we encourage that dialogue. Perhaps most importantly, we must do what we are doing today. We must talk openly and honestly about how we as Americans, black, white, and brown, can promote greater reconciliation and trust and greater access to the American Dream for all, so that there is more peace in our hearts and homes, schools and neighborhoods.

Again, I thank all of you for joining us here today to discuss the "tough stuff" of the Civil War. May a spirit of mutual respect and love govern your discussions.

Have a great conference and God Speed!

THE ROLE OF THE UNDERGROUND RAILROAD AS A CAUSE OF THE CIVIL WAR

SPENCER CREW

What I want to talk about this morning is the Underground Railroad as one of the steps along the road to the Civil War. This is interesting because the Underground Railroad is not necessarily an idea or a concept that first comes to mind when you think about the start of the Civil War. But if you go back to that time period, what you will find is that indeed there are people who are concerned about the Underground Railroad, noticing its activities and beginning to see it as an issue of concern.

For example, if you look at the words in 1859 of the Governor of South Carolina, William Gist, in his first presentation to the State Legislature as Governor, he talked about why South Carolina should think about seceding. Among the issues he raised, very specifically, was the issue of the Underground Railroad. He saw it as a scourge, and described it as an idea or a concept that was established to "assist our Negroes to escape from our service." For him it was one of "a string of Northern assaults on slavery [that were leading] towards outright war." In his mind, this institution and these activities were issues of concern. And he thought the Underground Railroad was one of those provocations that the

South should begin to consider as they were thinking about whether or not they should remain a part of the Union.

To hear him talk in this manner and to think about the Underground Railroad in this way is probably a little bit surprising. Often the depiction we have of the Underground Railroad is of a very low key, secret organization run by people operating in the shadows, not revealing who they were, and making their activities hard to detect. They were very guarded about how the system operated and where safe houses and hiding places were located. Their primary task was to support the efforts of enslaved African Americans seeking freedom. They sought to provide food, clothing, shelter, and direction to these brave souls on the run, but not to draw attention to themselves.

Often the Quakers are portrayed as a leading group in this effort because of their early involvement in this work. They were among the first to push for the abolition of slavery and the end of the slave trade. Because they were often low key and quiet about their work, the operations of the Underground Railroad are often associated with these characteristics as well. Levi Coffin is a wonderful example of this association. He is sometimes referred to as the "President of the Underground Railroad," as he and his wife, Catherine, operated for many years in both Indiana and Ohio. For many people the Coffins stood as the epitome of the work and the effort of those involved in the Underground Railroad.

But the Quakers were not the only ones active in the workings of the Underground Railroad. Others were involved as well, and many of them were African American. Frederick Douglass, Harriet Tubman, and William Still were all critical operatives in this operation, as runaways often went to the African-American community first because they felt it was the safest place to go. Frederick Douglass was particularly sympathetic to the plight of fugitives, as he had been a slave who escaped at a very early age using the Underground Railroad. He ran away from Baltimore headed northward and eventually became a stationmaster in the Underground Railroad, as well as a vocal and articulate critic of and spokesman against slavery.

His colleague in Underground Railroad activity was Harriet Tubman, whom we all know quite well. She gained notoriety because of her numerous trips south to Maryland, helping family and friends gain their freedom, because she felt that her having freedom alone was not sufficient. Her efforts caused great consternation in Maryland and throughout the South. She was the epitome of what slaveholders feared most: a fugitive slave returning to help other fugitives.

The high profile of people like Douglass and the notoriety of Tubman were reasons that the Underground Railroad was not always a low key activity. The actions of such well known individuals helped draw the attention of the residents of the North and the South to the activities of the Underground Railroad, as did some of the spectacular escapes that took place during this period. Two in particular are worth noting.

The first of these is what is referred to as the Nalle rescue. Charles Nalle lived in Albany, New York in 1860. Prior to that time he was an enslaved resident of Culpeper, Virginia and escaped by way of the Underground Railroad first to Washington, D.C., on to Philadelphia, and finally to Albany. We know this because William Still, who captured the words of many runaways in his book, *The Underground Railroad Records*, talked about Nalle coming to Philadelphia.

After leaving Philadelphia, Nalle settled quietly in Albany with the aid of local Underground Railroad operatives and anti-slavery forces in that city. He thought he was safe there and could lead a quiet life as a free man, but he was betrayed by a local official who knew of the reward for Nalle's return south and hoped to get it for himself. When he was arrested, Nalle was taken to the local sheriff's office, where a huge crowd assembled to rescue him. They eventually wrestled him away from the local officials and ran away with him. Among the people in the crowd was Harriet Tubman. Unfortunately, Nalle was recaptured, but the crowd freed him again, and he finally made his escape. You can imagine how this was seen. Among anti-slavery forces in the North, there was cause for celebration, but for pro-slavery residents living in the South and for Nalle's former slaveholder this was a matter of great concern over what the future might bring with regard to these issues.

The other escape to note is that of Henry "Box" Brown. Henry Brown lived in the city of Richmond, Virginia and traveled from Richmond to Philadelphia in 1849. He was aided by a couple of the citizens in Richmond in the building of a wooden box, nailing himself in that box, and then shipping himself to Philadelphia. The trip took 27 hours, traveling mainly by railroad. Part of that time he spent upside down, on his head. Brown said during this time he felt like his brains were falling out of his head.

After successfully arriving in Philadelphia, Brown began to give speeches around the country about his life in slavery and his escape from Virginia. At times he would stand on the box that he used to escape and talk about his experiences, thus standing as an illustration of the possibilities of freedom for those who were enslaved. More importantly, he stood as a symbol of disturbance for slaveholders. They were beginning to see a pattern developing in terms of people escaping and the organized presence of a system determined to undermine the institution of slavery. Both of these incidents increased the profile of and the publicity connected to the Underground Railroad. These incidents also give us a sense of how well-publicized these activities were.

Adding to the growing concern of slaveholders was the work of William Lloyd Garrison and his newspaper, *The Liberator*. On a regular basis Garrison highlighted activities connected with the Underground Railroad as well as famous rescues that were taking place. He did not give away the secret of how the networks operated, but he did publicize the incidents as a way to convey the desire of slaves to have their freedom. Garrison also wanted to generate support for the network of people who were determined to help runaways gain their freedom.

In the pages of his newspaper one could find the stories of people like Frederick Douglass and Harriet Tubman, as well as

William and Ellen Craft, who escaped from Georgia, traveled to Philadelphia, and eventually wound up living in Garrison's hometown of Boston. They did this by disguising themselves. Ellen, with her hair cut short, dressed as an ailing southern gentleman, and William played the role of "his" faithful slave, accompanying him northward. These escapes were the kind that Garrison loved to let people know about.

Also in the pages of his newspaper one could find the story of John Brown. Garrison did not necessarily condone what John Brown did, but certainly the idea of working against slavery was something he appreciated. John Brown was a longstanding active member of the Underground Railroad, and when he went to Harpers Ferry, one of the things he wanted to accomplish was the creation of a subterranean passageway, to provide fugitives easier access to the North and to freedom. For John Brown, this was one aggressive tactic the Underground Railroad and those who were opposed to slavery should undertake to fight against it.

Consequently, the activities of individuals like Garrison, Douglass, and Tubman, and other highly publicized successes of the underground participants, felt like a slap in the face to southerners, who believed their property rights were under attack. It also caused them concern about the future security of slavery given the direction they believed the nation was heading. The concern was strong enough that it became one of the often mentioned factors used by those considering secession.

I mentioned William Gist as one of those individuals, but there were others, such as Robert Hunter of Virginia, who served as Secretary of State of the Confederacy. Hunter pointed to the Underground Railroad as one of those factors compelling the South to break away. This concern was also expressed in other states throughout the South as they discussed people working against the Fugitive Slave Act of 1850. For them, these actions were reasons to leave the nation. They understood that the participants in the Underground Railroad sought to provide aid and comfort to runaways and to strike a blow against the institution of slavery. These southerners were cognizant that

Underground Railroad participants saw slavery as totally opposed to the ideals of the nation and hoped to bring about its destruction.

Ultimately, the Underground Railroad's efforts were disruptive enough to push slaveholders to consider breaking apart the Union. Control over their slaves was critical to the success of slaveholders. The Underground Railroad worked both to diminish the control of slaveholders and to undermine the argument that enslaved African-American people were content with their condition. Contented slaves would not run away. The Underground Railroad thus became another illustration of the opposing views of the North and the South about slavery, and further reason why southerners felt that secession was necessary.

Recognizing the above-ground publicity actively generated by the success of the Underground Railroad allows us to better understand its impact on southern thinking. For southerners, the Underground Railroad was another brick on the road that eventually led to the breaking apart of the Union. It also points out why the Underground Railroad can validly be seen as a factor in the start of the Civil War.

Waterways to Freedom: The Underground Railroad in Hampton Roads

Cassandra Newby-Alexander

When you think of the Underground Railroad, you think of iconic images, many of which appeared in Spencer's presentation, of Harriet Tubman and others, on foot, running away. But in reality, the vast majority of people who escaped did so aboard ship, and their escapes were concentrated in the period of the 1850s.

I would like to tell you a little bit about one particular story, and to focus on Norfolk, since we are here in Norfolk today. Spencer talked about Henry "Box" Brown, who was assisted by a man by the name of John Minkins. Minkins was a free black man from Norfolk working aboard the *City of Richmond* and other steamships that plied the seas between Richmond and Petersburg, Norfolk, Portsmouth, and on to Philadelphia. Henry Brown went by rail from Richmond, but Minkins passed through Norfolk on his way to freedom.

Slave owners sometimes posted notices for the return of fugitive slaves. One advertisement, published in the 1830s, mentioned a woman by the name of Hagar. She was an amazing person, based on the ad, because she was so determined to reunite with her loved ones, in particular her daughter, who had been sold away from her. Like many of the fugitive slave notices, up through the 1830s, this ad talked about the individual who escaped, and described her.

Twenty Five Dollars Reward.

HAGAR, a Negro Woman, about 30 years of age, rather a dark copper coloured Negro, slim and tall, say above the middle height, her head inclines forward from her shoulders more than customary, narrow visage, her mouth projects, nose pointed neither flat nor prominent, was sold about 3 years ago by Sam'l Hosier, (living near Nath'l P. Tatem's) to Andrew How, in Norfolk, and ran away in June last; Hagar has a daughter living with Wm. Jones, about 4 miles from Norfolk, off the road leading to Great Bridge, has been seen about N. P. Tatem's place, at Ferry Point and in Portsmouth—her mother-in-law's name is Prudence, living in Commerce Street.

All persons are warned against harboring her, and any person who will give information, or who will lodge her in jail, so that the subscriber can get her, shall receive the above reward.

J. B. Massieu, near the Court House, Mainstreet, Norfolk.

William Still, *The Underground Railroad*, Philadelphia, Porter & Coates, 1872.

Ads would refer to the fugitives' clothing; they would describe what fugitives looked like, where they were from, and where they thought these individuals had gone.

In the 1840s the port areas such as Norfolk and Richmond began growing exponentially, as did the number of escapes. One example was the case of George and Rebecca Latimer of Norfolk, the parents of the famous inventor and draftsman, Lewis Latimer. George and Rebecca Latimer decided to escape because Rebecca was pregnant and did not want her child to be born into slavery. This ad was different, because it revealed that two individuals ran away together, and it said that they left the area aboard a ship:

$50 Reward.

Ranaway from the subscriber last evening, negro Woman REBECCA, in company (as is supposed) with her husband, George Latimer, belonging to Mr. James B. Gray, of this place. She is about 20 years of age, dark mulatto or copper colored, good countenance, bland voice and self-possessed and easy in her manners when addressed.—She was married in February last and at this time obviously enceinte. She will in all probability endeavor to reach some one of the free States.

All persons are hereby cautioned against harboring said slave, and masters of vessels from carrying her from this port. The above reward will be paid upon delivery to MARY D. SAYER, Granby Street.

$50 Dollars Reward.

Ranaway on Monday night last my Negro Man George, commonly called George Latimer. He is about 5 feet 3 or 4 inches high, about 22 years of age, his complexion a bright yellow, is of a compact well made frame, and is rather silent and slow spoken.—I suspect that he went North Tuesday, and will give Fifty Dollars reward and pay all necessary expenses, if taken out of the State. Twenty Five Dollars reward will be given for his apprehension within the State.

His wife is also missing and I suspect that they went off together

JAMES B. GRAY.

William Still, *The Underground Railroad*, Philadelphia, Porter & Coates, 1872.

That was a critical difference. From the 1840s on, such ads told the public to be on the lookout for fugitive slaves on board ships. Of course, steamships left from Norfolk at least every single week. Where were they going? They were going to Philadelphia; they were going to Boston. They were eventually going to New York, to Syracuse, to New Bedford, Massachusetts, and many other places, and they were leaving regularly from this area.

Who assisted the fugitive slaves? Anyone who was either sympathetic to abolitionism or greedy enough to accept money in exchange for assistance with passage. What were some of the vehicles? What did they look like? One example is the steamship *Philadelphia* (below). There are records of a number of slaves who actually escaped aboard this particular vessel.

Steamship *U.S.S. Philadelphia*, 1859, drawn by Erik Heyl, 1956. U.S. Naval Historical Center.

What prompted them to escape? Auctions, sales; in some cases not it was not their own sale, but the sale of family and loved ones. In January in Norfolk, Portsmouth, Richmond, and other places, there were massive sales of people, not just one or two people, not just random sales, but thousands being sold every single year. Prior to January of each year, larger and larger numbers of people would flee. Usually it would be in October, November, or December, before the auction period, because most of the auctioneers would have the slaves removed from their masters and placed in a jail. Here in Norfolk it was Hall's Slave Jail, located where City Hall is today.

An ad for a slave auction (below) shows the amount of money they would usually charge, or at least hoped they would get, from the sale of each individual. This is important because it shows how valuable the internal slave trade was. A woman was valuable because of her ability to reproduce, and a man was valuable if he was a hard worker or if he had a skill or training. In Hampton Roads many people had skills because this was a port area.

During this time period, from the 1840s to the 1850s, there was a shift in the importance of the slave trade. Here in Virginia slave labor became a little less important than the slave trade itself. Some individuals were essentially helping people to reproduce so that they could sell their offspring into the slave trade going to the western parts of the South. As the nation expanded westward, laborers were needed, and Virginia was the supplier of a great many of those individuals. The reproduction rate was so high in Virginia that even as thousands of slaves were sent to the lower South, the population numbers here remained stable.

SALE OF NEGROES—By J. J. Moore & Co. on Saturday:

Woman 32 years, and child 10 months,	$850
Young Negro Man,	$1,190
Girl 13 years old,	$980

SALE OF NEGROES—On Saturday by Ferguson & Belote, auctioneers:

Mary Eliza	age 18,	825
Fanny	18,	1150
George	20,	1190
James	55,	300
Ann, aged 40 and child 6 months		600
Tom	14,	870
Sheppard	12,	675
Armstead	9,	561
Mary	6,	310

Transcribed from *The Southern Argus*, Norfolk, Virginia, 1859.

Also important was the fact that slave owners and traders were not only selling slaves but also hiring them out. Some eighty percent of women were hired out as domestic servants, cooks, laundresses, and midwives, and the men were hired out for port-related activities. This created a security risk, and suspicion first directed its lens at free blacks, so the rights of free blacks were increasingly constricted. But the lens started focusing on the slaves themselves, too. On the Underground Railroad many people who escaped were assisted by enslaved people hired out to work in the port areas.

After public attention focused on those who were assisting escapees, it began to focus as well on the fugitives themselves, who were escaping aboard the ships. One news article in *The Southern Argus* in Norfolk related how people were enticing slaves to run away.

CAGED—CHARGE OF ENTICING SLAVES.—On Friday a man named Cummings was arrested and taken before Charles H. Sheild, Esq., J. P., charged with being concerned in the escape of negroes, and also with selling books, &c., without a license. He was fined and imprisoned, and will have another hearing before the City Court at its next session.

Transcribed from *The Southern Argus*, January 17, 1859.

That was, of course, a lie. Enslaved people did not need to be enticed. The idea was that there must be some explanation, some rational reason, why these slaves who were so "happy," and I am speaking facetiously, would want to escape, so they must have been enticed to escape. We know that was really not the case.

By the 1850s fugitives started escaping in large groups. An example from William Still's book, *The Underground Railroad*, describes how six people escaped together. They were all from Portsmouth. By the way, most of them were members of a single church in Portsmouth, the Colored Methodist Church, now known as Emanuel AME Church. Several members of this group ended up fleeing to Canada and later returned to this country. This article shows that some of them were caught.

SENT UP.–Capt. Thomas Loveland and crew of the *Francis French*, went up to Smithfield yesterday, where they are to undergo trial for attempting to kidnap a negro.

Transcribed from *The Southern Argus*, Norfolk, Virginia, 1858

Even though the captain of the steamship *Francis French* was identified as the criminal in helping these slaves escape, it was the colored steward, William Thompson, who was thrown in jail. He was in prison all through the Civil War. He was not the only one. There were some white captains, like William Bayliss, who were also thrown in jail. There was one captain, Alfred Fountain, who was notoriously caught several times but somehow managed to avoid prison.

During this time there were groups of people who were identified as likely to help slaves escape: free blacks, skilled slaves who could move about without supervision, and white ship captains, who were seen as the greatest risk imaginable. Government officials and legislators made sure that these individuals would pay a heavy fine, or even pay with their lives, if they helped someone to escape. Officials provided incentives to the general population to identify those who were sympathetic to the escaping slaves. This newspaper article described fugitives

FUGITIVE ARRESTED.–We learn that on Sunday, Captain Southgate observed a likely negro girl on board his steamer, the Sea Bird, on the trip down from Hampton, and found on inquiry, that she had left Hampton, (where she is owned) in charge of a negro slave residing in Norfolk, and as the affair was not satisfactory to Capt. S., he placed them in charge of the proper officer, who took them to jail.

Transcribed from *The Southern Argus*, Norfolk, Virginia, 1859.

who were arrested because someone noticed them getting aboard a vessel.

The captors got reward money not only from the individual slaveholder but also from the state. What was the problem here? Millions of dollars in enslaved labor was leaving the area. It was disrupting the social order and the economy. There were inspection laws established, too, among other efforts made to catch slaves.

Hundreds of slaves escaped through Norfolk, and these numbers were concentrated in the 1850s. Slaveholders knew that friends and family had lost enslaved labor to the Underground Railroad, and they became paranoid, not just in this area but throughout the South. They were on edge, fearing that a neighbor, a friend, or someone nearby might cause them to lose their property, money, and status in society.

The Underground Railroad really generated the feeling among southern slaveholders that they must stop what was going on. By the time of the Civil War, the Underground Railroad was definitely an important factor that helped to stir up this fear, this sense among slaveholders that the South must separate in order to preserve slavery.

THE QUEST FOR BLACK RIGHTS IN THE MIDST OF WAR

EDNA GREENE MEDFORD

My two colleagues have ably described the process and motivation for African Americans attempting to free themselves before the war. We now turn to a discussion of African-American activism during the war years. African Americans greeted the news of southern secession and eventually war with hopeful anticipation. Unlike those who favored compromise, people of color welcomed the fight for its potential to alter their standing in American society. "God Speed the conflict," declared the New York based *Anglo-African*. "Out of this strife will come freedom." If others were slow to recognize the impact the war could have on slavery, African Americans knew it would, as Frederick Douglass suggested, "deal a death blow to the monster evil of the 19th Century." But Douglass and others in the black community defined freedom more broadly than simply the destruction of slavery.

The fortunes of all black people had been inextricably linked to the most disadvantaged among them. The privileged few could expect little effort from whites to recognize their rights as long as slavery defined the entire race, but African Americans knew that even with the death of the institution, true freedom would have to be won by dismantling social and legal practices of long standing. Hence, ending slavery and securing unabridged citizenship became the twin goals they sought.

On the eve of the war, black men and women assailed the universality of prejudice and discrimination in America. "Some people think we are oppressed only in the South," explained John Rock, a prominent Boston physician, lawyer and abolitionist. "This is a mistake. We are oppressed everywhere in this slavery cursed land." Rock and other black leaders railed against the denial of the elective franchise in many northern states. They condemned the practice of sending African-American children to inferior, segregated educational facilities, and the barring of blacks from certain public accommodations and places of entertainment. They were especially aggrieved by the inability of many to pursue a decent living. Even the highly skilled and well educated found it difficult to acquire jobs that would enable them to take care of their families. So while some donned the Union blue to destroy slavery, those left behind fought on the home front against custom and legislation that singled them out for abuse.

Nowhere was the abuse of black people more pronounced than in the "land of Lincoln," where laws and practice proved hostile to both enslaved and free blacks. Although counted among the free states, Illinois permitted slavery under certain circumstances and allowed the owners of enslaved people to retrieve their runaways. Local newspapers featured fugitive slave notices that offered rewards for the capture and return of runaways, and jurisdictions were authorized to apprehend such persons and jail them until their owners could be located. And this was in the free state of Illinois. Free people of color endured black laws that barred them from voting or holding public office, from serving on juries and testifying against whites in court, and that required them to show evidence of freedom. Illinois, like Indiana, prohibited the immigration of free blacks. The statute had been in effect for some time, but the war years saw its vigorous enforcement.

During the war, John Jones, a wealthy Chicago tailor, launched a campaign to overturn the state's black laws, especially anti-immigration legislation. Jones and a group of prominent black Chicagoans organized the Repeal Association and placed their grievances before the state legislature. "We have been treated as strangers in the land of our birth," they argued. "We ask only evenhanded justice and all of our wrongs will be at an end by virtue of that act." As a result of their efforts, Illinois repealed the offending laws in February of 1865. But neighboring Indiana retained its black laws until after the war.

In other areas of the North, the fight for equal rights centered on disparate treatment of streetcar passengers. In Philadelphia, for example, African Americans were prohibited from riding in the interior of the cars and were only allowed on the front platform, if at all. The campaign in Philadelphia was led by William Still of Underground Railroad fame. With the support of the Social, Civil, and Statistical Association of the Colored People of Pennsylvania, Still repeatedly petitioned the streetcar companies for repeal of their policy against black ridership. In late 1864 the group petitioned again, citing the fact that African Americans—law abiding, taxpaying residents of the city—suffered insult and abuse at the hands of local whites, encouraged by the existence of such degrading practices. The petition alluded to the service that black men were rendering to the nation, while their brothers and sisters were denied equal access to public conveyances.

Still was joined in the struggle for equal rights in Pennsylvania by Octavius Catto, the highly educated son of prominent parents in the local African-American community. Catto accepted no limitations on his or any other black person's aspirations. Whether the issue was equal access to the streetcars or the right to vote, he pressed for full and unconditional citizenship for his people. For all of his effort, Catto was murdered in 1871 by a disgruntled Democrat who was alarmed at black voters and their support for the Republican Party.

Understanding the value of education in the quest for a better future for their children led African Americans to agitate as well against inferior segregated schools throughout the North and the West. Taxpaying parents, especially wealthier ones, rejected the notion that their children should be relegated to overcrowded, ill-kept facilities, or in some areas, enjoy no public education at all.

In Rhode Island the campaign for desegregation of the public schools won the support of restaurateur George Downing, a lifelong champion of full equality. At age fourteen he had helped to organize a literary society whose members pledged to abstain from observing the Fourth of July because the Declaration of Independence gave African Americans very little to celebrate. As an adult he became an active participant in anti-slavery societies and pre-war conventions held for racial uplift and the promotion of equality. An ardent critic of separation of the races, he led the effort to desegregate the public schools in Newport after his own children were denied equal access to education. Newport schools were not desegregated until after the war, but the efforts of Downing and others like him hastened integration's arrival.

In those areas of the North where black men were denied equal political voice, African Americans agitated for complete and unconditional enfranchisement. Leaders such as Frederick Douglass understood that true freedom was possible only if black men could protect their interests through the political process. Douglass and other black New Yorkers had pressed in 1860 for repeal of discriminatory voting rights legislation in that state.

With the war now underway, Douglass asserted that black men's service to the Union cause entitled them to the rights of citizenship. As encouragement to black men to serve, he counseled: "Once let the black man get upon his person the brass letters U.S., let him get an eagle on his button and a musket on his shoulder and bullets in his pocket, and there is no power on Earth which can deny that he has earned the right of citizenship in the United States."

The quest for voting rights was not limited to the North. Black men in the Union-occupied South petitioned Lincoln to intervene on their behalf in their struggle for the franchise. The President obliged on April 11, 1865 in what would be his last address. He stated publicly what he had already suggested in private—that voting rights should be extended to educated black men and those who had served the Union as soldiers. That fact always gives me pause. No one was talking about whether or not uneducated white men could vote, but black men would have to be educated in order to qualify to vote.

Douglass presided over the premier national drive for the promotion of equal rights for African Americans during the war. Delegates from eighteen states, including seven southern states (Virginia, North Carolina, South Carolina, Florida, Mississippi, Louisiana and Tennessee) attended the National Convention of Colored Citizens of the United States, held in Syracuse, New York in October 1864.

The 144 men who assembled issued a declaration of rights that included a demand for the "immediate and unconditional abolition of slavery," the right to resist colonization outside of the U.S., and enjoyment of the full rights of citizens. "We claim that we are by right entitled to respect," their declaration began, "the immunities and privileges of all other citizens and defenders of the nation should be conceded to us. We claim the right to be heard in the halls of Congress and we claim our fair share of the public domain." Before adjourning, the delegates formed the National Equal Rights League, which, in addition to encouraging education, temperance, and thrift, aimed to persuade white Americans of the rightness of their cause.

The quest for equal rights during the war years did not reflect a departure from traditional activism. Rather, it was a continuation of the long struggle that African Americans had engaged in throughout the first half of the nineteenth century when they met at annual conventions to assess their condition and plot a course for redressing their grievances. But during the war, the quest was accompanied by a sense of urgency, by the recognition that as they were on the threshold of crushing slavery and because they were helping to preserve the Union, the time might be at hand when they could secure their birthright.

They were not immediately successful on every front; it would take constitutional amendments and special legislation to complete the work they had begun, but their victories encouraged them in the belief that true freedom was attainable. Even John Rock, who had railed against the discrimination that had pervaded the North, could point to personal triumphs during the war years. In February of 1865, with the help of Massachusetts Senator Charles Sumner, Rock became the first African-American lawyer admitted to practice before the U.S. Supreme Court. It was in many ways a victory for all people of color, since eight years earlier, in the Dred Scott decision, the proslavery court had rejected the idea of African-American citizenship. Now one of the dispossessed would take his place at the bar of justice in the highest court of the land.

Black Soldiers and the Struggle for Equality during the American Civil War

IRA BERLIN

The Civil War transformed American society. For no one was this more true than the four million enslaved men and women of African descent. In the course of less than six years, from the beginning of the war in 1861 to the beginning of Radical Reconstruction in 1867, some four million black people went from slavery—literally defined as property—to free; to soldiers in the world's most powerful and ultimately victorious army; to citizens of the world's greatest Republic; to elected leaders of that Republic. One can imagine how those who experienced those extraordinary changes came to believe they could change the world. The revolutionary transformation that accompanied the Civil War and the post-war Reconstruction empowered men and women to believe they could remake American society as they believed it should be.

The black men who served as soldiers and sailors in the Union Army and Navy felt the war's revolutionary effect. Soldiering transformed black men, their families, their communities, and eventually the entirety of American society, white as well as black, North as well as South. I would like to briefly discuss some of the soldiers' experiences and their impact on African-American life and on American life.

The Emancipation Proclamation of January 1, 1863, invited black men to join the Union Army and Navy. They had been pleading for the opportunity since the war began, and early in 1863, Secretary of War Edwin M. Stanton authorized the recruitment of black men in the North, beginning with the enlistment of the Massachusetts 54th and then 55th, as well as black regiments in Connecticut and Rhode Island. Although the majority of these men had been free, some for several generations, in the North, fugitives from the South could be found among the ranks of these free state regiments. Soon thereafter, Stanton moved to expand the enlistment to include slave men in the Union-occupied South. Eventually, more than two hundred thousand black men would serve in the Union Army and Navy, and they would compose ten percent of those who served in the northern armed forces. Their presence was critical to Union victory.

The incorporation of black soldiers into Union ranks at once turned to northern advantage, and it enhanced the antislavery character of the war. The liberating force of black enlistment weakened slavery in the loyal border states and the Union-occupied South no less than in the Confederacy, thereby extending the nation's commitment to freedom beyond the limits of the Emancipation Proclamation. Black enlistees in the border states, which had been exempted from the liberating provisions of the Emancipation Proclamation, received their freedom, and, eventually, their enlistment also guaranteed the liberty of their immediate families. Throughout the slave states, black enlistment and slave emancipation advanced together and, indeed, became inseparable.

Black men coveted the liberator's role, but soldiering remained a complex, ambiguous experience. Once enlisted, ex-slaves who yearned to confront their former masters on terms of equality found themselves enmeshed in another white-dominated hierarchy, which, like the one they had escaped, generally assumed their inferiority. Organized into separate black regiments, paid at a lower rate than white soldiers, denied the opportunity to become commissioned officers, often ill-used by commanders whose mode of discipline resembled that of slave masters, and frequently assigned to menial duties rather than combat, black soldiers learned forcefully of the continued inequities of American life.

Nonetheless, the war left black soldiers with far more than their freedom. They gained new skills in regimental schools and a wider knowledge of the world in army service. Fighting and dying for the Union advanced the claims of black men to all the rights and privileges of citizenship. Victory over those who had previously dominated their lives bred a confidence that soldiers proudly carried into freedom and that permeated the entire black community. The successes of black soldiers in their war against discrimination within the army, however limited, politicized them and their families, preparing all black people for the larger struggle they would face at war's end.

Once enlisted, black soldiers had much in common with Billy Yank or even Johnny Reb. They experienced the same desperate loneliness of men fearful for their lives and separated from family and friends. The same reveille blasted them from their bunks in the morning, and the same tattoo put them to bed at night; the same mosquitoes invaded their tents in the summer and the same wind whistled through their barracks in the winter. Like white soldiers, they enlisted expecting the glory of great battles but often found themselves wielding shovels rather than rifles. They too grumbled about long hours on the drill field, complained about overbearing officers, and bemoaned the quality of army rations. And, like soldiers everywhere, they found relief in the camaraderie of the campfire.

Yet, if military life created countless similarities among soldiers, the seemingly insoluble distinctions between slave and free, black and white, nevertheless remained. When black soldiers first entered the Union Army, federal officials—from Secretary of War Stanton to local recruiters—assured them that those who fought under the American flag would enjoy its full protection and benefits. But those promises were soon broken at every turn. No federal official ever gave serious consideration to placing white and black soldiers in the same units. Black enlistees were denied the right to rise within the ranks, paid less than white soldiers, used as uniformed menials rather than soldiers, and, if captured, treated as rebels-in-arms rather than prisoners-of-war. Instead of speeding black people down the road to equality, federal policies confirmed the established American pattern of invidious racial distinctions.

One federal policy, however, proved particularly obnoxious to black soldiers, their families, and the entire black community. Pay discrimination became the center of a massive struggle between black soldiers and the federal government for whom they fought. It provoked prolonged protests by black soldiers and their abolitionist allies and captured the attention of the northern public. Believing the assurances of the early army recruiters and recruitment broadsides, black enlistees assumed that they would receive the same remuneration as white soldiers. But the War Department ruled that the legal basis for black military service lay in the 1862 Militia Act and paid all black soldiers according to its provisions: $10 per month, minus $3 for clothing, rather than the $13 per month, plus clothing, that white privates received. Even black commissioned and noncommissioned officers received the same $7 monthly pay, so that the highest-ranking black officer earned barely half the compensation of the lowest-ranking white enlisted man.

Unequal pay angered black soldiers. The reduced income imposed a severe strain on families dependent upon black soldiers for their support, but the principle mattered at least as much. Black men in the army, those recruiting soldiers, and those contemplating enlistment, as well as advocates in the anti-slavery movement, attacked the discriminatory pay policy as yet another vestige of second-class citizenship. Led by black soldiers recruited in the free states and encouraged by sympathetic white officers, several regiments refused to accept the $7 monthly pittance, regarding it as an affront to the dignity of an American soldier. Rather than submit to inferior treatment, some went more than a year without pay. The 54th and 55th Massachusetts regiments even refused Governor John Andrew's offer to use state funds to increase their compensation to the amount white privates received. In the meantime, they fought and died, dug fortifications and fell ill, and fumed at the progressive impoverishment of their families. In late 1863, the protest boiled over in open revolt. Black soldiers in the 3rd South Carolina Infantry, led by Sergeant William Walker, stacked their arms and refused to perform duty until the army granted equal pay. Walker's superiors charged him with mutiny and executed him as an example to other black protesters. But Walker's death did not stem the protest. Instead, black soldiers stationed in other parts of the South began to agitate for change. Many teetered on the brink of mutiny until Congress passed an act equalizing the pay of black and white soldiers in June 1864.

The question of pay not only set black soldiers apart from white soldiers, but also encouraged black soldiers to make common cause amongst themselves. Although they wore the same uniforms as white soldiers, observed the same articles of war, answered to the same system of military justice, and confronted the same enemy, black soldiers fought a different war. Because they struggled to end inequality as well as to save the Union, they faced enemies on two fronts, battling against the blue as well as the gray to achieve their own freedom and that of their people.

The struggle for equality within the Union Army taught important lessons. Not only did congressional provision for equal pay and the War Department's tardy acquiescence on the question of commissioning black officers stir optimism about eventual equality, but the struggle itself awakened men previously excluded from the political process to the possibilities of redressing their grievances, informed them of the means by which their goals might be achieved, and identified the federal government as a forum for obtaining justice. Northern free blacks had a long tradition of political protest, which they drew on freely and passed quickly to slave soldiers, most of whom had no formal political experience. Before long, regiments composed of newly liberated slaves petitioned and protested with all the skill and tenacity of those whose members had been born free, demanding that the government recognize its earlier promise of equal treatment and provide them and their families the dignity and protection due all American citizens. In so doing, former slaves learned something about the system of government under which Americans lived. They came to understand that justice depended not on the favor of a single powerful individual but on impersonal rules and regulations that governed all citizens.

Soldiering thus provided black men with more than legal freedom. In dramatic and undeniable ways military service countered the degradation that had undermined black self-esteem during the antebellum years. Battlefield confrontations with the slaveholding enemy exhilarated black soldiers by demonstrating in the most elemental manner the essential equality of men. But nothing more fully reveals the revolutionary impact of soldiering on black life than the transit of black men from slaves to liberators. In smashing the manacles that bound their people, black soldiers elevated themselves and transformed their own consciousness. In their own eyes, in the eyes of the black community, and, however reluctantly, in the eyes of the nation, black men gained a new standing by donning the Union blue and participating in the nation's great triumph.

The black military experience also affected many black people who never wore the Union uniform. From the moment of enlistment, military service altered the lives of black soldiers' families. In some places, enlistment of the head of the family—husband or father—ensured the families' safety and secured their freedom. In the border states, where slavery was unimpeached by the Emancipation Proclamation, the enlistment of husbands and fathers established the only claim to liberty for many soldiers' families.

Elsewhere, black soldiers guarded contraband camps and Union-held plantations to prevent Confederate raiders from recapturing and re-enslaving loved ones. But the same act of enlistment that provided protection for some black families encouraged the abuse and confinement of others. Angry masters who vowed to take revenge upon women and children whose husbands, sons, and fathers dared to enlist had little compunction about making good on their threats.

After enlistment, the experience of black soldiers continued to shape the lives of those who remained behind. The questions of equal pay and protection, which appeared in the guise of abstract justice to interested white people, touched the wives and children of black soldiers in a direct and immediate manner. After all, the treatment accorded black prisoners was a matter of life and death, and the difference between $13 and $7 per month was the difference between subsistence and starvation for many black families. By the same token, the impoverished condition of families left at home or liable to abuse by Confederate guerrillas or former masters influenced the conduct of black soldiers. Nothing more surely moved them to protest than news of the material hardship or physical suffering of their families.

The accomplishments of black soldiers reverberated beyond the family circle. Black soldiers eagerly bore the news of emancipation. In carrying freedom's sword, they demonstrated that liberty was as much the product of the black man's valor as it was the white man's gift. Slaves understood this, and they welcomed black soldiers with special enthusiasm. Fugitives followed the soldiers' line of march; bondsmen and women, fearful of their owners' wrath, sought refuge with black regiments; and everywhere crowds of black men, women, and children lined the roads to cheer.

Besides bearing the message of liberty, black soldiers also aided the passage of black people from slavery to freedom in countless practical ways. They informed freedpeople of their newly won rights, tutored them in the nuances of federal policy, and elaborated on the opportunities that liberty offered. Although the message they carried—like the rumored possibility of land—often proved to be an empty promise, it encouraged freedpeople to press their former owners and, indeed, their new Yankee rulers in ways that expanded freedom.

The influence of soldiering on black life did not end when the shooting stopped. If anything, its importance grew. Many black soldiers remained in uniform as part of the Union Army of occupation, and they continued to advise freedpeople on the new demands of freedom and the workings of the world beyond the plantation. Their presence, especially when commanded by sympathetic white officers, helped to limit violence against freedpeople and to prevent newly returned Confederate veterans from riding roughshod over defenseless former slaves. Military service also provided a stepping stone to leadership in the black community. With wartime responsibilities behind them, black soldiers became deeply involved in the black communities where they were stationed. Some took wives from among the local population and fully entered local community life, thereby fusing the experience of the liberator and the liberated. Drawing on their martial experience and the confidence it engendered, black soldiers framed the aspirations of many of the newly freed and also helped reconstruct the black community's institutions to meet the demands of freedom. They frequently took the lead in establishing schools, building churches, and founding fraternal societies.

In the first political conventions held by black people following the war, soldiers played a prominent part. By standing armed and ready to aid black people, and by bringing knowledge and confidence to their communities, black soldiers remained significant figures in a world they had helped to turn upside down.

THE MYTH OF BLACK CONFEDERATES

BRUCE LEVINE

Popular views of the American Civil War are rife with myths, and one of the most energetically propagated and widely accepted of those myths concerns the so-called "Black Confederate" soldiers. According to this myth, anywhere from ten thousand to a hundred thousand southern blacks, both free and slave, served voluntarily and loyally as full-fledged combat soldiers in the South's armies. Whole units, we are sometimes told, of black Confederate troops confronted Union Armies from the very start of the war.

None of these claims is small: ten to twenty thousand soldiers would add up to more than ten full-strength infantry regiments, and fifty thousand soldiers would be enough to fill out four full-strength infantry divisions. Numbers much greater than fifty thousand troops would approximate the size of Robert E. Lee's entire Army of Northern Virginia on the eve of Antietam.

Those who most aggressively assert these claims generally do so to buttress another even bigger one, namely that, to quote one of these online opinions, "most blacks supported the Confederacy," that, indeed, "the overwhelming majority of blacks . . . supported and defended with armed resistance the cause of southern independence."

Now, the Confederate war effort did depend upon the labor of its black population in many forms. Southern states and armies impressed, which is to say forced, many thousands of enslaved men and women, as well as free blacks, to build and maintain fortifications, emplace artillery, drive wagons, play music, tend horses, cook meals, wash clothes, dig graves, and so on. Some slaves served as personal servants to white soldiers. It was not unusual for such slaves to be given uniforms, and occasionally one of them even picked up and fired his master's musket at northern soldiers, thereby perhaps winning for himself some additional approval and trust from the white Confederate soldiers all around him.

In a few places, free blacks in the South sought to prove their loyalty to the South and shield themselves from suspicions that they were Union sympathizers by enrolling in local home guard and militia units that were not part of the regular Confederate forces. A handful of light-skinned men managed to slip unnoticed into regular infantry units by concealing their African ancestry and passing for white.

All of these things are well-known facts. They are not controversial. Nobody that I know of denies them.

What is not a fact and what the vast majority of trained Civil War historians know is false is the claim that large numbers of black southerners served in the Confederate Army as soldiers. In fact, in 1861 neither the Union nor the Confederate governments would allow non-whites to serve as soldiers. Lincoln, as we know, changed course. But the Confederacy stood firmly by its ban on black troops during the first 46 of the war's total 48 months, until the spring of 1865, until just a few weeks before the Confederacy's final defeat and destruction. Until that point of extremity, the South wanted no slaves, indeed wanted no men at all who were not certifiably white, under arms. Its leaders said so repeatedly.

Right after the Battle of Bull Run/Manassas, one Confederate general did advise Jefferson Davis to emancipate and arm slaves, but Davis vehemently rejected that advice. It would,

Davis reportedly snapped, "revolt and disgust the whole South." And two years later in late 1863 when asked whether a group of well-to-do men of "mixed blood" in Alabama might form a Confederate regiment, Secretary of War James Seddon replied that only those who were obviously white would be allowed to don the gray. Those who could not be clearly, in Seddon's words, "disconnected from Negroes" could not enlist. They could only be used as non-soldier military laborers. And Seddon reaffirmed that policy in November of 1864.

So why was the Confederate leadership so stubborn on this score? Because it was fighting to preserve the slavery of millions of African Americans. It feared, quite logically, that placing black men under arms would undermine slavery, both in theory and practice. Central to the justification for slavery, after all, was the assertion that black people were inferior, and being inferior, they would make poor soldier material. As Secretary of War Seddon put it, that stance, which the Confederacy had taken both before "the North and before the world," did "not allow the employment as armed soldiers of Negroes."

Confederates refused to employ blacks, and especially slaves, as soldiers for other and more practical reasons. They feared, for one thing, what black troops would do. Secretary of State Judah P. Benjamin, for example, worried that black Confederates would desert "in mass" to the enemy, and there was good reason to think he was right, because that is precisely what happened when Confederates ordered slaves to perform non-combat labor in support of their armies. Confederate General Joseph E. Johnston summarized the result toward the close of the war in a private letter to a close friend. "We have never been able to keep the impressed Negroes with an Army near the enemy," he said, because "they desert." If unarmed laborers deserted to the enemy, what might armed black soldiers do with their weapons, if given the chance?

The Confederate leadership's policy of excluding blacks from its armed forces was effective. John Beauchamp Jones, who was a high-level assistant to the Secretary of War, scoffed at rumors that the Confederacy had slaves in its armies. "This is utterly untrue," he noted in his private diary in March of 1863. "We have no armed slaves to fight for us." Months later, asked to double-check, Secretary of War Seddon confirmed, "No slaves have been employed by the [Confederate] Government except as cooks or nurses in hospitals and for labor."

At the beginning of 1864, a number of officers in the South's second biggest army, the Army of Tennessee, recognized the Confederacy's serious shortage of soldiers and shortage of likely reinforcements. So they urged Richmond to re-examine its policy—to offer to free and arm male slaves who would fight against the Union. Jefferson Davis, again, forcefully and promptly rejected that proposal. In fact, he ordered an end to all discussion of that proposal in the Confederate Army because the very idea of putting black men in gray uniforms was too inflammatory to air publicly.

But by the end of that year, Davis recognized that the Confederacy's military situation had become so dire that it was necessary to reverse himself and endorse a version of that proposal. That decision of his provoked a stormy war of words that dominated the South's political life for the next six months. His critics reminded him that blacks could not make good soldiers, or if they could make good soldiers, they would fight against the wrong soldiers, or they would simply desert and take their weapons with them to the enemy.

In response to these criticisms, Davis and his supporters now had to convince the skeptics that black soldiers might be induced to fight effectively and loyally for the South after all. The way they argued this point, or did not argue this point, is interesting, because in trying to make the case they never pointed proudly to the record of any of the black Confederate brigades or regiments or companies or even lone individuals that today's propagators of the "Black Confederates" myth claim were already in the field. They could not point to them because they did not exist.

Finally, in March of 1865, after a great deal of arm twisting, a watered-down version of Davis' proposal finally became Confederate law. General Richard S. Ewell assumed

responsibility for implementing it. Confederate leaders and
Confederate journalists confidently predicted the enlistment of
thousands. The actual results fell far short of those projections. One
dwarf company or two of black hospital workers was attached
to a unit of the Richmond home guard just a few weeks before
the surrender at Appomattox. The regular Confederate Army
managed to raise maybe forty to sixty men. And the way the
Army treated those forty to sixty men is interesting, too. It
drilled them, fed them, housed them at military prison facilities
and placed them under the command of military police officers
and prison wardens, demonstrating a deep distrust of their
newly recruited black soldiers. This strikingly unsuccessful last-
ditch effort, furthermore, constituted the single, sole exception
to the Confederacy's otherwise consistent refusal to enlist
African Americans as soldiers. As General Richard Ewell's long-
time aid-de-camp, Major George Campbell Brown later noted,
this small group of black soldiers mustered in Richmond in the
last weeks of the war were "the first and only black troops used
on our side."

It is fitting to let the former slave, Frederick Douglass,
explain why the great mass of slaves declined to respond to
Jefferson Davis's offer. They turned their backs on that offer,
Douglass wrote, because it "called upon the Negro for help to
fight against the freedom which he so longed to find, for the
bondage he would escape." It called on him to "fight against
Lincoln, the Emancipator, for Davis, the enslaver." To expect
any appreciable number of black men to respond enthusiasti-
cally to any such proposal, Douglass concluded, was a species of
"madness."

PANEL I DISCUSSION

Panel I: James O. Horton, Ira Berlin, Spencer Crew, Bruce Levine, Edna Greene Medford, and Cassandra Newby-Alexander.

JAMES HORTON I am reminded of an interesting story about the reach of the Civil War. For the last five years, for one semester a year, I have been teaching at the University of Hawaii, where I did some research on Lincoln and found that Lincoln had significant connections with several Hawaiian kings. Lincoln became very popular in Hawaii, and one result of that is that when the Civil War began, Hawaiian people participated. Lincoln got a letter from a merchant in Hawaii saying that he had put together a militia. He offered that militia unit to Lincoln to fight for the Union cause. Very few people know about this.

I found also a letter written by Samuel Armstrong, a white man who was born in Maui. As you know, the African-American regiments all had white officers, and Armstrong became an officer in an African-American regiment, and one of the things he wrote was that many of the Hawaiian soldiers in the Union Army joined African-American regiments. After the war was over, Armstrong helped to establish Hampton Institute, a college for African Americans, now known as Hampton University. He taught there for a while, and one of his students was Booker T. Washington.

Now, panelists, if you would like to address any of the things
that your fellow panelists have talked about, you can do that.
We have about ten minutes.

SPENCER CREW Well, I had a couple of thoughts as I was
listening to Edna's and Ira's presentations and noticing the
names that began to pop up. It struck me how engaged these
individuals were, not only in activities for civil rights in the
North where they were located, but so many of them were
activists in the Underground Railroad. John Jones in Chicago
was a key player in the Underground Railroad. I began to see
straight-line connections between these individuals that
continuously fueled their civil rights activism before, during,
and after the war. I found it intriguing.

EDNA GREENE MEDFORD Too frequently we assume that
there is a disconnect, that African Americans are just involved
in the Underground Railroad before the war and then they
switch to trying to help in the struggle to end slavery by going
into the military, when the reality is they are doing both at the
same time throughout the first half of the nineteenth century
and into the war years as well. These are people who believe
in freedom, and freedom is very broadly defined.

And, so, yes, they are concerned about their brothers and
sisters in the South who are still enslaved, but they are also
concerned about making sure that the rights of citizenship are
extended to those people in the South once they are freed as
well, and concerned about extending those rights for
themselves, because they don't have those rights in the North,
either, for the most part.

IRA BERLIN The point Edna makes, and the overall discussion
of the Underground Railroad, raise a profound question of
the chronology of the Civil War. We say that the Civil War
begins at Fort Sumter, but clearly the struggle for freedom
begins earlier. If we look at the Underground Railroad, this
emancipation of black people in the South, this self-
emancipation, this community emancipation, rattles through
both the black community and the slaveholding community.

At the very same moment when some are aiding black

people to escape from the South, others, slave catchers, are being sent to the North to retake fugitive slaves or even take people who are free and drag them into slavery. Throughout the 1850s, the investments of slaveowners are protected by federal legislation in the form of the Fugitive Slave Act.

There's a kind of war going on, and struggles often break out into violence. People are killed or maimed or traumatized in these conflicts. Our understanding of the Civil War and emancipation needs to be stretched with regard to how we bracket the war years.

CASSANDRA NEWBY-ALEXANDER   It was in New Bedford where the 54th Massachusetts regiment was organized, and New Bedford is the place where so many fugitives escaped to. William Carney, for example, went from Norfolk up to New Bedford, where he enlisted in the 54th Massachusetts regiment. Another person, Thomas Bayne—his name was Sam Nixon while he was a slave—joined the 54th, and he was actually a conductor on the Underground Railroad here in Norfolk.

When the war ended he, like a lot of people, returned home and entered politics. He was a representative to the Virginia Convention, rewriting the Constitution in 1867 and 1868. So this whole idea of this confluence of ideas and history and people really was important during this particular period.

IRA BERLIN   If we look at who enlists in those first regiments, we find that they are fugitive slaves, people who escaped and can't wait to sign up. They can't wait to get even. They are anxious to meet their former masters on the field of battle.

EDNA GREENE MEDFORD   At the same time you have men who had never been enslaved who are living in the North saying, "Yes, we are willing to go fight for the freedom of these enslaved people, but you had better give me my rights at home before I do anything for the Union." They are adamant about that throughout the North, and they are pressing, for instance, the state of Michigan, to get rid of all those laws that suggest that black people are inferior.

BRUCE LEVINE One of these men, an escaped slave, brings up another aspect of this that I would like to pay more attention to. His name was Garland White and he was a slave of Robert Toombs, one of the most politically influential men in Georgia. Garland White escapes while Toombs is in Washington, D.C., and makes his way North, possibly with the assistance of William Seward. White doesn't stop in the North but goes on to Canada. We have no written record of why he did that, but we're reminded by a number of things fellow historians have written, if we didn't know already, that it is dangerous to be a fugitive slave in the North, precisely because there are people in the North who are willing to help with the recapture of fugitive slaves.

I would like to ask how many fugitive slaves went to Canada and whether anybody on the panel knows whether there is a fluctuation in the tendency to stay in the North or go on? Last point: once the war begins, Garland White follows the news of the war in the newspapers. Once it is safe to come back, he goes to Ohio and becomes a minister. As soon as the North begins to allow black men into the army, he joins one of the first regiments, recruits a whole bunch of others, and is one of the first men to march into Richmond.

JAMES HORTON Spencer Crew mentioned William and Ellen Craft, and remember that Ellen Craft disguised herself as William's master to make their escape to Boston. Today, one stop on the Black Heritage Trail in Boston is a home that was owned by Lewis Hayden, who was born a slave, escaped from Kentucky, went to Boston, and became very much involved in the anti-slavery movement and the Underground Railroad there.

When the Crafts got to Boston, they hid out in Lewis Hayden's house. If you look at the U.S. Census for 1850, you will find that William and Ellen Craft are listed as living in Lewis Hayden's house. Can you imagine that fugitive slaves are listed in the census? These are shocking things, but they make this kind of research very, very interesting.

When doing research in Hawaii, I ran into the story of a

fugitive slave named Anthony Allen, who had escaped with the assistance of a sea captain. He signed on to a whaling ship, which eventually went to Honolulu, where he jumped ship and he became part of King Kamehameha's inter-island ferry service. He served as a sailor on that ferry service and stayed in Hawaii for the rest of his life. In my research I found a letter that Anthony Allen was writing to his former master's son. I can imagine him sitting on the beach writing about life in Hawaii. One of the things he reports to his former master's son is that he has married two Hawaiian women—and this is a direct quote—"as is the custom."

If you ever go to Honolulu, be sure to go to the corner of King and Punahou Streets. Incidentally, our current President, Barack Obama, went to Punahou School, four and a half blocks away. At the corner of King and Punahou, you will find a school that was built on the land that was owned by Anthony Allen. So now you have a good reason to go to Hawaii for your research.

PANEL I
QUESTION & ANSWER SESSION

Moderator: William Alexander, Professor of History at Norfolk State University. Panel I: James O. Horton, Ira Berlin, Spencer Crew, Bruce Levine, Edna Greene Medford, and Cassandra Newby-Alexander. Questions were submitted by audience members and live bloggers and via Twitter, Facebook, and email.

WILLIAM ALEXANDER We are going to start with a question that I think is sufficiently broad as to cover the entire topic of the session, and to be addressed to all of the panelists. Did race identify free blacks with the same status as enslaved people in white society, particularly during the period up to the Civil War and also during the Civil War? How did this affect the free blacks' role before entering the war?

In other words, what about the intersection of race and slavery? Was there a clear delineation or was one really influenced by the other?

IRA BERLIN I'll take a first shot and hopefully others will join in. What we can say in the largest perspective is that there was a great tension within free black life. In 1860 there were about a half a million free blacks divided roughly between the free states and the slave states. There were slightly more free blacks in the slave states.

I don't think there is much doubt that northern free blacks are completely identified with the cause of the slave. They are agents of the Underground Railroad. They speak to the question of equality. There's a profound understanding that their own quest for equality, which is severely circumscribed in the northern society where they are denied many of the rights of citizenship, the right to vote in almost all places, the right to sit on a jury, the right to testify in court, the right to travel freely, all of those things as free blacks, that their great quest for equality is limited by the existence of slavery and that ending slavery would speed them down the road to full American citizenship.

In the South it becomes more complicated because free people of color, as they are sometimes called, speaking to mixed racial origins, are viewed with enormous suspicion. Slaveholders, understanding that their own position rests upon racial unity, that all white people support the slave cause, presume the same thing is true about all black people, that free blacks (or free people of color) in the South will stand with the slaves. Indeed, they'll be the agents of insurrection. That is, the people who have freedom to move about, some education, and a little bit of wealth, will be the leaders of a slave insurrection. So their lives are particularly prescribed, not simply all of those prescriptions that I mentioned for the northern free blacks, but others as well.

If you are a successful free black in the South, you then are in a very, very difficult position. How can you demonstrate that you are okay to the white community, a white community that might turn on you at any time, at which point you'll need some help? You'll need some powerful white guy, some powerful slave owner to step forward and say "He is okay; you can trust him." One way to do that is to identify with the slaveholding class in manners of speech, in manners of deportment, in terms of where you live, in terms of whom you interact with. You don't want to be seen identifying with slaves.

Perhaps the best way to prove your loyalty to the slaveholding state is to own slaves yourself. So we see that many of the best positioned, wealthiest free people of color in the South are themselves slaveholders. These are people under enormous difficulty and that difficulty is somehow manifested in a variety of behaviors.

When the Civil War comes, many of these free people of color will join native guard units, will volunteer to help with the Confederacy. But as soon as the Union Army arrives, they switch their gray uniforms to blue and are in a very different position.

So, the place of free people of color is a complicated one. It has a lot to do with where you are, who you are, and what your origins are in this society. I guess I would start there.

SPENCER CREW It strikes me how complicated "free" is, particularly in the North and particularly with regard to the Fugitive Slave Act of 1850, which complicated the lives of African Americans living in the North. They had been free for a long time and suddenly they realized that, according to their heritage and lineage, they might not, in fact, be free, or they might have a family member who was not free. It became a complicated issue because the definition changed.

I think also many free African Americans are writing letters back to the South and communicating, so there is this strong bond with friends and relatives who are still living in the South. The community has a freewheeling conversation back and forth, and the definitions of free and slave are murky, as states grapple with slavery between the North and South and who is legally free and who is not. It makes everything much less clear-cut than it might be otherwise.

JAMES HORTON One of the things that Spencer is saying is that there was generally a strong connection between slaves and free blacks. We're talking about four million slaves and about a half a million free blacks, and the chances of a free black person not having a relative or a friend who was a slave was very, very low. There was very little possibility for African Americans who were free to be completely disconnected from people who were enslaved.

And about free blacks who owned slaves in the South: It was a good thing to own slaves because it would give you some leverage and perhaps some advantages with the white population. But it's interesting to look at who owned whom.

A lot of people owned their children and their husbands or wives. They owned people in their family. That is so they could say, "Yes, I'm a slaveholder" and get some advantages from the white population, and at the same time make sure that their relatives, their kids, their spouse were well taken care of. If your son is to be owned by somebody, if you are concerned about that, why not have him owned by you, so you can make sure he is safe?

Those are the kinds of issues that were often very difficult to deal with, especially after the Fugitive Slave Act of 1850. You did not have a right to self-defense if you were accused of being a slave. You did not have a right to a lawyer or a jury trial. Therefore, you could be accused of being a slave and taken into slavery even if you were free.

So these were very difficult times for free blacks as well. That's part of the reason that the Underground Railroad was becoming extremely significant after 1850.

EDNA GREENE MEDFORD Even in the South there were laws that demanded that free blacks and enslaved people were not to come together. They were not to go to the same churches and if there was a black church there had to be a white person present to make sure that the free blacks were not plotting with the slaves.

But even with those laws, free blacks and enslaved people came together and interacted to the point where in many areas enslaved people were not allowed to control the grains. They had been milling the grain and short-changing the white customers and giving the rest, the surplus, to free black people. So there were many connections between the two groups.

CASSANDRA NEWBY-ALEXANDER I would also mention that the Fugitive Slave Act really provided incentive for people to identify slaves. State laws provided further incentive by offering rewards if you turned in people or captured a fugitive slave. There were many free blacks in both the North and the South who were kidnapped into slavery.

If you ever have a chance to read Solomon Northup's

Twelve Years a Slave, this is what he talked about. He described his journey to Washington, D.C., to try to get a job, and from there to Richmond to Norfolk and then farther south to Louisiana. He encountered many free blacks who were kidnapped, beaten up, and imprisoned, and he was himself imprisoned and sold into slavery.

These developments started changing the attitudes of free blacks, who had thought freedom guaranteed them actual freedom and found out it didn't. Because they were black, their freedom was always on the verge of being lost. So many free blacks who before 1850 may not have been so concerned about slavery, after 1850 became very concerned and decided that freedom for everyone was the only way to protect themselves.

EDNA GREENE MEDFORD Some of those who went to Canada agitated for freedom from there. They didn't just leave the country and forget that there were people left behind who did not have freedom. They continued the struggle.

WILLIAM ALEXANDER Speaking of the Underground Railroad, we had several questions on that topic. One had to do with the impact of the Underground Railroad enlightening northerners about the realities of slavery, and perhaps one or two of you could comment on that. The other part of the question is this: How did the slaveholders in the South feel about the impact of the Underground Railroad as they were thinking about secession? Did they believe that they could do away with the Underground Railroad, perhaps that would be possible through secession, or did they make that connection?

CASSANDRA NEWBY-ALEXANDER I would like to point again to the story of George and Rebecca Latimer, whose narratives were used by abolitionists in Boston to campaign against slavery, humanizing enslaved people and exposing the atrocities of the institution.

And, of course, we know that Frederick Douglass became the prime example of a brilliant, scholarly person who had in fact been enslaved. One reason he wrote *The Narrative of the Life of Frederick Douglass* was to show that he had been enslaved. Opponents wanted to prove that he was not a slave so that they could somehow destroy the abolitionists' argument that intelligent people had been enslaved.

I'm sure you have some more to add to that, Spencer, but the Underground Railroad really generated suspicion among southerners in general, and particularly slaveholders. They believed there was a national conspiracy. While there were a number of people in the North and the South guiding fugitive slaves to freedom, the connections to one another were loose.

Still, the idea that there was an Underground Railroad conspiracy helped to fuel this southern paranoia. Whenever Congress started talking about abolitionism and slavery, slaveholders became fearful that slavery would eventually be destroyed.

SPENCER CREW Having been in Ohio for the last four or five years, I have come to understand that in all the border states there were active networks of Underground Railroad that weren't so much below ground. Levi Coffin in Indiana, a free state, was not afraid to stand forward and say "If they come to me, I will help them."

Thomas Garrett was renowned for having been taken to court for having helped a husband, wife, and two children gain their freedom, being fined in a way that almost cost him his land, and then in the end saying, "I consider this a license that I am paying for. If you have anyone to be free, send them to me."

So, there exists a more public positioning by individuals involved with the Underground Railroad, and I think it does increase slaveholders' concerns. In Maryland, they didn't know for sure if it was Harriet Tubman, but there began to be paranoia, with laws being passed and also lots of action going forward. We believe there was a bounty put out for Harriet Tubman, and the public was increasingly aware that Underground Railroad activists were going to the South and bringing people back.

The publicity increased the awareness of the people in the South and the North with these narratives in the newspapers and other public media.

BRUCE LEVINE On the subject of paranoia, you just need to look at the statements explaining secession. Featured over and over again is the idea that northerners are facilitating the escape of "our" property. Jefferson Davis, when he writes his after-the-fact history of the Civil War, insists that slavery wasn't the cause of the war and lists what the South's real concerns were. Once again, there is the complaint that northerners are letting our slaves get away and violating our property rights.

This is magnified when a series of northern states begin to pass so-called personal liberty laws that are meant to provide fugitives with the rights that the Fugitive Slave Act denied them.

In other cases, governments in the North mandate that northern officials take no part in assisting the capture of slaves. This is just an outrage in the South and proves to them, once again, that they are connected in this Union to a people who are not going to help them hold onto their property.

IRA BERLIN In any system of tyranny, the aim of people who are running that system is to make it airtight, to eliminate the contradictions. That's what makes the Underground Railroad so significant, such a great concern to slaveholders. That's why they want to eliminate free blacks. They want to re-enslave free blacks. That's why they want to open up the slave trade, to make the identity between blackness and slavery, whiteness and freedom, uniform and complete, so there are no contradictions. And the Underground Railroad undermined this.

I would like to add one thing, a caution that I always start with, when sharing my thoughts on history in the South. When we talk about "the South," we have to be careful whom we are talking about. When a student says "the South supported slavery," it seems obvious until we remember that four million people in the South, who were very much southerners, were actually opposed to slavery. We should speak instead of slaveholding southerners, to distinguish them from slaves, who were also southerners, and had lots of opinions about the institution of slavery, which for the most part were not favorable.

CASSANDRA NEWBY-ALEXANDER I want to add one more thing. When people think about the Underground Railroad, they think of it as a total package. They don't realize that the majority of people who escaped, escaped from the upper South and from those areas that are bordering the North. There are a few examples of people coming from the lower South, but they came mostly from the upper South.

What makes it even more dramatic is that the entire South was consumed with this paranoia that there was a national conspiracy to spirit away the slaves. In point of fact, most of the South wasn't even affected by the Underground Railroad, but it happened to be in the areas where the population was greatest, and that was the upper South.

JAMES HORTON Or in the part of the South with ports, with connections to water, because a lot of slaves made their escape aboard ship. If you weren't close to the northern states, you might still have real advantage if you were near a port, because you might be able to get aboard a ship and make an escape in that way.

SPENCER CREW I think it's important to add that we often think about the Underground Railroad as going north, and it's not always about the North. Especially when you think about ships, it is going to the Caribbean, it is going to Mexico, it is going sometimes to England. It is finding a way to escape the bondage of slavery and going wherever you can get. Most often it is North, but as Professor Newby-Alexander pointed out, the ships go everyplace. If they get on the ships, they are going anywhere.

JAMES HORTON They are going to freedom, not to any particular place.

WILLIAM ALEXANDER This is a three-part question about the black Confederates, for Bruce. Who is most responsible for promulgating the myth of the black Confederates? Who particularly benefited from the perpetuation of the myth? How has this controversy affected the public memory of the Civil War?

BRUCE LEVINE I think it's pretty clear to anybody who just Googles the phrase "black Confederates" that this idea is mostly put forward by so-called Confederate heritage organizations, who are determined to prove, first, that slavery wasn't the cause of the Civil War, and if you push a little further, they sometimes offer the idea that slavery wasn't really so bad, as "proved" by the claim that all these thousands and thousands of slaves were loyally defending their masters.

There is a definite agenda attached to these claims. It is not always the same agenda, because there is, as with everything else, a sort of sliding scale of extremism on the point. Generally, those who press the point hardest and most determinedly and will not hear evidence to the contrary are those who are most determined to prove that slavery was extraneous to the war and that supposedly the great majority of the black people in the South were loyal to the Confederacy. They are the same people who have benefited from the spread of this myth.

There are cloned websites all across the country. One is almost identical to another, filled with misrepresentations, and sometimes with cropped photographs. A case that Professor Horton likes is a photo that appeared not long ago on the Web purporting to show a black Confederate unit in Louisiana (page 62). It turned out this was only a portion of an original photograph. The original, larger photograph shows that these soldiers are in fact standing next to a Union officer, because this group is part of the Union Army.

That is only the most obvious example of the series of misrepresentations which, dare I say, makes one wonder how sincere are some of those accusations and how agenda-driven

A cropped and captioned image used as evidence of a
black Confederate Army regiment.

The original photo of a Union Army regiment, taken in a studio in Philadelphia.

many of them really are. They have been remarkably successful in confusing a large portion of our population on this subject. There is even a Defense Department website that claimed that this was true. There's a lot of work to be done in rolling back these misunderstandings.

JAMES HORTON The fact that there is a white officer standing there in a dark blue uniform makes it clear that these are Union soldiers. That's very interesting. And it's even more complicated because this picture was the model for a painting that was used as a Union Army recruiting poster for African Americans. In the poster they use the painting, but they added the American flag flying over and people cheering the troops on.

So not only does it not depict Confederate soldiers, but this picture was used to recruit black Union soldiers.

WILLIAM ALEXANDER Unfortunately time is not going to be on our side. Our question time is up. Let me, first of all, thank the panelists. Are there any questions from the panel? We have about half a minute.

JAMES HORTON I'll do this in half a minute. You heard Bruce Levine talk about the laws that were set up in the North called personal liberty laws. These laws were passed in Massachusetts, New York, and Pennsylvania, saying that state facilities and personnel could not be used in the capture and return of slaves. Now, obviously the southern slaveholders were well opposed to that and they wanted to make sure that the Fugitive Slave Act was enforced.

Occasionally you hear people argue this: the Civil War wasn't about slavery; the Civil War was about states' rights. What they say is that those people who were willing to go to war were committed to the idea that states have the right to set up provisions and laws, and those laws cannot be superseded by the federal government.

I was challenged on that assertion once, and I answered with this challenge: Find me an example of a Confederate leader or hero or person who is substantially significant in the

Confederacy who would say, "I am opposed to the Fugitive Slave Act because it overrides the personal liberty laws passed by individual states. I am for states' rights, so I think those states have the right to pass personal liberty laws. I am opposed to the Fugitive Slave Act because it overrides states' rights." Find me one person who has said that and I'll take the states' rights argument seriously, but I have not found a single person.

Slavery, Freedom, and the Union Navy

James McPherson

Most students of the Civil War and of African-American history are familiar with the story of Robert Smalls. On May 13, 1862, this South Carolina slave brought the Confederate armed dispatch steamship *Planter* out of Charleston carrying fifteen other slaves, including his and his brother's families, and turned the *Planter* over to the Union blockade fleet. This daring escape received wide publicity in the North and made Smalls one of the first black war heroes. He signed on as a pilot for the Union fleet in South Carolina waters, and went on to become a leader of the Republican Party in low-country South Carolina and served four and a half terms in Congress during the postwar era.

Smalls' exploit was spectacular, but in many respects not unique. Although no other slaves who escaped Union ships brought such a valuable prize as the *Planter*, many of them paddled away from slavery in skiffs, scows, dinghies, rafts, or canoes. Just two weeks before Smalls steamed past Fort Sumter's frowning guns, fifteen "fine contrabands," in the words of Flag Officer Samuel Francis Du Pont, commander of the South Atlantic Blockading Squadron, had appropriated Confederate General Roswell Ripley's barge and rowed it out to the Union fleet at night. They had belonged to the Quartermaster's Department in Charleston, and according to Du Pont they provided him with important information on "the various defenses, forts, entrenchments, bridges, etc." in the region. They also brought the intelligence that three blockade runners laden with cotton were set to run out and six runners were due in from Nassau laden with war material for the Confederacy. "This information," wrote Commander John Marchand of the *U.S.S. James Adger*, senior officer on the Charleston blockade, caused him "to alter the positions of the blockading vessels" for better advantage. Like Robert Smalls, several of these fifteen "contrabands" were skilled watermen and pilots who became valuable to the Union fleet as free men.

Smalls told Du Pont that the Confederates had abandoned their outer defenses in the Stono River, a sort of back door to Charleston. Du Pont sent several gunboats into the river while planters on James Island desperately tried to remove their slaves to the mainland. Commander Marchand described the ensuing scene on May 21st, 1862:

> About 4:00 in the afternoon, we heard the most horrific screams ashore, the lookouts at the masthead having previously reported a stampede on the cotton and corn fields to the south of the river. A company of [Confederate] cavalry then was seen to emerge from the pines ... charging at full speed amongst the flying slaves ... [firing] their pistols on all sides amongst the Negroes ... so I directed the gunboats to open fire on the mounted men and a half a dozen shells ... [sent them] scampering in every direction.

The gunboats took on seventy-one of the black fugitives; within three days several hundred more had come in. Ships took them to Port Royal, where they joined the thousands of other freedpeople on the Sea Islands who had been liberated by Du Pont's fleet the previous November.

From the beginning of the war, slaves had voted with their feet for freedom by escaping to Union lines. In May 1861, Major General Benjamin Butler at Fort Monroe in Virginia, just across the roadstead, Hampton Roads, had refused to return three fugitives who had escaped by boat from Norfolk. He refused to return them to their Confederate owners, labeling them as "contraband of war," liable to seizure as enemy property being used to wage war against the United States. Both the label of contraband and the policy initiated by Butler stuck. By the war's end, at least half a million contrabands had come within Union lines. They had achieved freedom by various acts of Congress, by Lincoln's Emancipation Proclamation, and most of all by their own actions and those of Union military personnel on the ground.

When we say that slaves achieved freedom by coming within Union lines, our vision of such "lines" is of army camps and garrisons and the perimeters of occupied territory held by soldiers. And indeed, most of those half million contrabands did achieve freedom by coming within those perimeters or by the advancing Union armies driving away the enemy and occupying an enlarged perimeter. But when we think about this process, what we may not visualize is the advance of the Union Navy into the estuaries, bays, coves, harbors, and rivers of the South. Only about five percent of the Union armed forces were in the Navy. But just as the Navy made a much greater than five percent contribution to ultimate Northern victory, so was the Navy the primary instrument in the liberation of far more than five percent of the contrabands who came within Union lines.

It was the Navy that often penetrated earlier and more deeply than the Army into the Tidewater regions of the South Atlantic and Gulf coasts, into the valleys of the lower Mississippi River and its tributaries where much of the slave population lived. It was Du Pont's fleet that captured Port Royal in November 1861 and thereby liberated 10,000 slaves on the South Carolina and Georgia Sea Islands. It was Flag Officer David G. Farragut's fleet that captured New Orleans and opened the lower Mississippi Valley to Union occupation in 1862. It was river gunboats that captured Memphis in June 1862, and they played a vital role in the campaign that captured Vicksburg a year later. And these were just the largest and best known of scores of campaigns by what Lincoln called "Uncle Sam's web-feet." "At all the watery margins they have been present," said the president in August 1863, "not only on the deep sea, the broad bay, and the rapid river, but also up the narrow, muddy bayou; and wherever the ground was a little damp they have been, and made their tracks."

At all of these watery margins, slaves made their tracks to Mr. Lincoln's gunboats. Volume four of the *Official Records of the Navies in the Civil War* is full of references to slaves who hailed gunboats of the Union's Potomac Flotilla in the summer of 1861 and were taken aboard in groups of four, ten, thirteen, twenty-three, and so on. Ship captains deluged Secretary of the Navy Gideon Welles with questions about what to do with these people. In September 1861 Welles responded, "The Department finds it necessary to adopt a regulation with respect to the large and increasing number of persons of color, commonly known as contrabands, now subsisted at the Navy yards and on board ships of war." They could not be returned to slavery and could not be supported indefinitely by the government. "You are therefore authorized," Welles went on, "when their service can be made useful, to enlist them for the naval service, under the same forms and regulations as apply to other enlistments."

The same message went out from Welles to Du Pont and to the naval officers on the Mississippi. "The large number of persons known as 'contrabands' flocking to the protection of the United States flag," Welles told Flag Officer Charles H. Davis of the Western River Flotilla in April 1862, "affords an opportunity to provide in every department of the ship, especially for boats' crews, acclimated labor. The flag officers are required to obtain the services of these persons for the country by enlisting them freely in the Navy."

The Navy was a year ahead of the Union Army in recruiting contrabands. For the war as a whole, the Navy enlisted twice the percentage of its personnel (about seventeen percent) from this manpower pool than did the Army. By 1863, Acting Rear Admiral David D. Porter, commander of the Mississippi Squadron, was recruiting hundreds of contrabands as firemen, coal heavers, and even gun crews on his gunboats. "The light-draft vessels have only half crews," he reported to Welles, so "I am making up deficiencies with contrabands as fast as I can." Porter was pleased with his black sailors. "They do first rate, and are far better behaved than their masters," he declared. "What injustice to these poor people, to say that they are fit only for slaves. They are better than the white people here, who I look upon as brutes, and half savages." A lieutenant commander under Farragut discovered that "the able-bodied negro makes a good artillery man" on shipboard. "In the working of the great guns, for coolness, quickness in handling the rammers, sponges, powder, shot, and shell, I found that they were exceedingly apt, and fond of it."

These officers had certainly not been abolitionists before the war. They belonged to one of the most conservative, even aristocratic professions in the antebellum era. If there was an aristocracy in America, Samuel Francis Du Pont, grandson of a French royalist who had been forced to emigrate during the French Revolution, was a member of it. Although not a slaveholder himself, Du Pont had always been a defender of slavery. But, as with many others, the war turned him into a convert to abolition. "I have never been an abolitionist," Du Pont confessed during the war, "on the contrary, most of my life a sturdy conservative on the vexed question . . . defended it all over the world, argued for it as patriarchal in its tendencies," he wrote in 1861. "Oh, my! What a delusion. . . . The degradation, overwork, and ill treatment of the slaves in the cotton states is greater than I deemed possible, while the capacity of the Negro for improvement is higher than I believed." Not an officer in his squadron had voted for Lincoln in 1860, Du Pont noted in April 1862, but now, he said, "there is not a pro-slavery man among them."

The same could not be said of any comparable group of Union Army officers at that stage of the war. Du Pont was especially impressed with the courage shown by the contrabands who risked their lives to escape. "No danger deters them," he wrote, "and they encounter shooting with perfect composure." Du Pont hired several of these men as pilots, in addition to Robert Smalls. He declared that they "have shown the utmost skill in piloting the gunboats and this under fire too—generally smiling and showing their white teeth when a shell exploded over their heads, while many [white pilots] brought up to the business didn't show their white teeth." Perhaps the white teeth of black pilots and the tensely compressed lips of white pilots can be seen for some kind of metaphor for the revolution of freedom wrought by the Civil War. We cannot say that the Union Navy carried through this revolution all by itself, but we can say that without the presence of Uncle Sam's webbed feet at all the watery margins of the South, the revolution would not have come as soon or so thoroughly.

John Washington: How, When, Where, and Why Emancipation Happened

David W. Blight

Obviously we are on the eve of the 150th anniversary of the Civil War, and there are many ways of thinking about it. But here is one way of thinking about it. During the centennial of the Civil War, I would suggest that the greatest Civil War centennial speech or moment was the speech Martin Luther King, Jr. gave on August 28th, 1963 at the Lincoln Memorial, known always as the "Dream Speech."

But the dream did not come until the very end of the speech. The dream metaphor was one of only five different metaphors or refrains that King used brilliantly in that speech. Five times in the first paragraph he said, "five score years ago," playing on Lincoln's use of "fourscore" in the Gettysburg Address a hundred years earlier. The entire framing of the Dream Speech was the Civil War and the emancipation centennial. The other refrains he used repeatedly in that speech were refrains like, "no, we are not satisfied," "with this faith," as he said about four times over, or, "let freedom ring," which he said several times over.

This morning I was reminded of that when someone made a reference to King's famous metaphor of the promissory note of the Declaration of Independence. The Dream Speech is an

John Washington (center) and family, Cohasset, Massachusetts, c1918. Alice Jackson Stuart Family Trust

iconic moment that children learn in a usually sanitized atmosphere now where they do not even know what the event was about. It was all about the hundredth anniversary of the Civil War.

But as an example of the actual emancipation in the Civil War, few stories are better than that of John Washington. His is a Virginia story of a heretofore unknown American slave who escaped in the midst of the war, because of the war, and because of the presence of Union forces. John Washington was born a slave in 1838 in Fredericksburg, Virginia. His father was a white man, though John never knew who his father was, and I and a research assistant have never been able to figure out the identity of his father. It is not the easiest thing to find ancestors named "Washington" with specificity in central Virginia.

His mother was a slave woman named Sarah, later Sarah Tucker. His mother was literate, and he learned his alphabet and first letters from her, which was one of the first lucky breaks of John Washington's life. He lived for quite a while, from ages nine to roughly twelve, on a farm west of Fredericksburg. John had some experience as a boy of growing up on a farm, but primarily he was an urban slave. And that has nearly everything to do with why and how he ended up escaping.

He came back to Fredericksburg. He saw his mother for what he thought was the last time, and his narrative includes the moment that all male slave narratives possess, the last time he sees his mother, or so he thought when it happened.

When he was twelve his mother was rented or hired out along with his four half siblings to Staunton, Virginia, over in the Valley. He did not see his mother again until after he escaped from slavery to Washington, D.C. in 1862. John's story is this: he was very talented, very skilled. He was literate. And already when he was a teenager, his owner, a Ms. Taliaferro (the ownership of John Washington is complicated, but he ended up owned by a Ms. Taliaferro by the mid- to late 1850s) began to hire him out.

He was hired out first as a jack-of-all-trades to a family for a year. He drove their wagon, he fixed everything, and he cleaned their yard. He was hired out for a while to a tobacco factory in Fredericksburg.

He worked a year in that tobacco factory which he said he really liked because it had nothing but routine. And that may sound strange to us, but for John it was twelve hours a day. Sometimes he could work fourteen hours a day, and he would get to keep the money from the extra hours, plus he said he liked the routine, because in his normal life with Ms. Taliaferro as a boy he had been forced to follow her around with a stool. She would make him sit on the stool, always within her eyesight, so that he would be at her beck and call. He said at the tobacco factory there was no Ms. Taliaferro, there was no stool, and he got to twist the tobacco. He said it was the first time he had ever heard the Negro work songs, and he loved them. He had heard the spirituals at church but he never heard the work songs.

He was hired out finally to a tavern in Richmond, which was owned by a Greek immigrant and later by a German immigrant. It turns out Virginia was pretty diverse even in the

Civil War era. He spent a year in Richmond, 1860 into 1861, working in this tavern where he described the Confederate forces coming into the capital at the beginning of the war, and walking in the city as though something really big was about to happen. And John avidly read newspapers.

He came back to Fredericksburg in the winter of 1861 to 1862 because he was engaged to a young woman he had met at black church fairs. Her name was Annie Gordon. She was about four years younger than John and she was free. John married Annie in January 1862. They were married by a white minister who was known to marry black people in Fredericksburg, which was not that uncommon.

Then John Washington refused to take the next hiring out back in Richmond that his owner demanded. He stayed in Fredericksburg and was hired out to a hotel called the Shakespeare, where his job was, in a way, an assistant manager. When the Yankees arrived in April of 1862, they took Falmouth, and they were about to take Fredericksburg. Everyone was evacuating the city and in John's narrative he described all the white people evacuating Fredericksburg and the white guests at the hotel escaping. The owner of the hotel came up to him that morning, handed him a wad of cash, and said, "John, pay off the help with this money and then do what you must."

John took all the black help, about a dozen people, up onto the roof of the hotel, which was about two blocks from the Rappahannock, where they could see across the river, and they observed what he called "the gleam of the Yankees' bayonets." Then he brought all the twelve workers down into the kitchen, and, as he told us in his narrative, he poured a round of drinks and held a toast "to the Yankees." Then he said to his co-workers, "Get out of here but don't get too far from the Yankees."

John Washington walked out of the Shakespeare Hotel and down to the riverfront with his cousin. He watched the formal surrender of the city. He saw the bridges burning and then he walked upriver. He walked toward the sound of a Union band, and then he crossed the river at Ficklin's Mill. The old stone

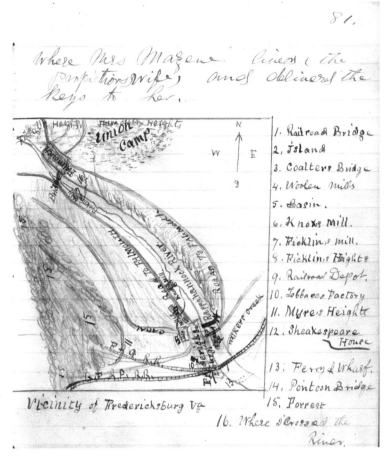

ruins of that mill are still there. The National Park Service, I am delighted to say, is now commemorating this event as part of their public tours.

John Washington drew a map (above) to record his moment of freedom, which is significant because as far as I know there is no other such extant document of a former slave who chose this way to record the moment of his freedom in the narrative he wrote after the war. It is a map of Fredericksburg, of the Rappahannock River, with sixteen places and names. He provided a map key, listing all the significant places, such as the

Shakespeare Hotel and Ficklin's Mill. They are all there so that someday, whoever would read this document would have a guide, a map of the day he became free—the most important day in his life.

He crossed the Rappahannock in a rowboat and encountered the officers of a New York regiment. Right near Falmouth, on the 18th of April, John was asked by a Union officer, "Would you like to be free?" Washington wrote, "My response was, by all means!" That night he slept in the camp of a New York regiment, and the next day he witnessed the burial of seven Union troops who had died to take Falmouth. In the narrative Washington wrote that the clods of dirt hitting their coffins were the first sounds of his freedom.

John Washington spent the rest of that summer with the Union Army as a guide and a mess cook. He was part of the Union forces right through the Second Manassas campaign. He dated his entry into Washington, D.C. as part of the first wave of freedmen into the District as September 1, 1862. I first picked him up in a city directory in 1864. He had his wife, his newborn child, his mother, and his grandmother, Molly, with him living at the same address, where today stands Constitution Hall. John lived out the rest of his life in Washington, D.C., or most of it. He is buried in Cohasset, Massachusetts, which is another part of the story time does not permit me to tell.

I knew it was possible to find descendants of John Washington, because his sons had children. Through the persistence of my brilliant research assistant and some help from Google, we eventually found Ruth Washington. Ruth is now in her nineties, a retired teacher who lives in Tampa, Florida. I had the out-of-body experience of calling Ruth in the fall of 2008 to tell her that I was about to publish her grandfather's autobiography. It took a while on the phone. It was a moment of confusion and disbelief: "You're doing what?"

By the end of the evening, she warmed up to the news, and we have become friends. Never say never about the connections of African-American families to the stories of slavery. She knew nothing about her grandfather until we were able to give her the book and tell her the story, which she embraced fully. She came to Fredericksburg, where she was presented with the key to the city, spoke in a church next to me, and signed all the books (see Further Reading, page 135).

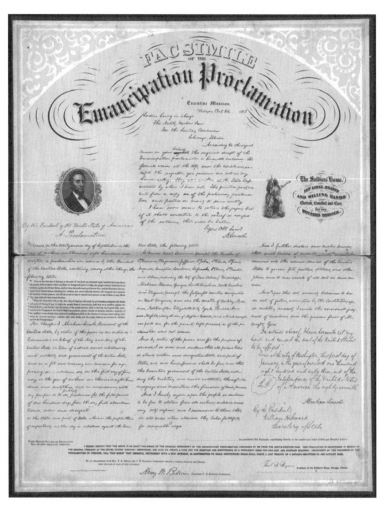

Ed. Mendel, Thomas B. Bryan, Chicago, 1863. Library of Congress, Alfred Whital Stern Collection of Lincolniana.

THE IMAGE OF THE EMANCIPATION PROCLAMATION IN ART AND MEMORY

HAROLD HOLZER

Jim Horton spoke this morning and again this afternoon about contradictions in history and complications in memory. I would like to explore some of them as they relate to Abraham Lincoln and the way in which he was viewed in his time, not just now, but the evolution of his reputation as emancipator and liberator, its limits, its boundaries, and its highest efflorescence. We have to look at the way he was treated at the time to get a good idea of the public response to emancipation. I am going to do it not in words, but through pictures. We start with the text of the Proclamation.

For about six months, President Obama had on display in the Oval Office a copy of a special edition of the Emancipation Proclamation. He took veterans of the civil rights movement to view it on Martin Luther King, Jr. Day. I wonder how many people knew, including the President, that it was one of a limited edition, struck right after the Proclamation's issuance. Autographed editions were offered at the Philadelphia Sanitary Fair for ten dollars each. Most of them did not sell.

Emancipation as a relic was not immediately popular. One reproduction of the autographed document (page 78) was donated by Lincoln to a Chicago charity fair in 1863. It sold for

$5,000 to a local entrepreneur, who promptly recycled it as a lithograph and sold it popularly. By the way, Lincoln won a gold watch for donating the most valuable object, and in those days of nondisclosure he kept it, wore it, and was happy with it.

The easiest way for commercially driven illustrators to depict emancipation at the beginning was by using the words. As you know, the words of the Proclamation are legalistic. They are not particularly inspiring. One publisher, Max Rosenthal, took his emancipation image (below) to the White House and gave it to Abraham Lincoln. Rosenthal was so entrepreneurial that he then produced an image of Lincoln examining his print (page 81), and made it into an advertising leaflet. Lincoln called such efforts "ingenious nonsense."

Max Rosenthal, L. Franklin Smith, Philadelphia, 1863. Library of Congress, Alfred Whital Stern Collection of Lincolniana.

PROCLAMATION OF EMANCIPATION.

THE SECOND OF
DECLARATION INDEPENDENCE!

BY PRESIDENT LINCOLN.
JANUARY 1st, 1863.

In presenting to the public, the Liberty-loving people of the United States, this elegant historical memorial, we feel that no comment is needed upon its great and noble subject, the undying parchment that sealed to Fame the name of our beloved Martyr-President, that made Abraham Lincoln the great liberator of a race, that made 1863 a great era in the history of the Republic, and wiped away the great stain that for eighty years had darkened its glorious annals. It is undying and immortal, beloved and revered, and further comment is unnecessary.

A suitable copy or memento of this great document should be and will be in the house of every lover of his country. One finer or better adapted to the demands of the public than this, we hesitate not to say, has not yet been produced. In beauty of design, artistic finish, and yet within the means of all, it is unsurpassed.

SUN, LIBERTY, EAGLE, NATIONAL BANNERS.

GEORGE WASHINGTON,

Benjamin Franklin,	Thomas Jefferson,
Chief Justice Story,	John Quincy Adams,
John Wesley,	William Penn.
Lucretia Mott,	L. Maria Child.

ABRAHAM LINCOLN,

William H. Seward,	Horace Greely,
Salmon P. Chase,	Charles Sumner,
James H. Lane,	Cassius M. Clay,
John S C. Abbott,	Wm. H. Burleigh.

JOHN C. FREMONT,

Wendell Phillips,	Owen Lovejoy,
Rev. Nathan Brown,	H. Ward Beecher,
Benjamin F. Butler,	Gerrit Smith,

Ten Vignettes, Representing the Curse of Slavery and Blessings of Liberty.

Fury, Satan, Calhoun and Jeff Davis.
Plantation Scene.
Slave, Auction, Separation.
Branding Slaves, C. S. on forehead, Barbarism.
Goddess of Liberty, Upas Tree, Slave, Hounds.
Purity, Dove, Olive Branch.
School.
Happy Family, Restoration.
Church, House, Plowing, Civilization.
Justice, Man, Railroad, Steamboat, Ship.

The Proclamation is on fine plate paper, 20 by 26 inches, appropriately and beautifully colored, 32 portraits; in all, over 120 figures, with descriptive pamphlets sent to any address by mail; postage paid on receipt of $2.00.

The Greatest Novelty of the Age! The Proclamation of Emancipation Illustrated !!

Card Photograph containing 721 words, 10 vignettes, 38 Portraits, and over 124 figures, should adorn every loyal lady's Album. *Price 20 Cents.*

LITHOGRAPHED BY ROSENTHAL, AND PUBLISHED BY L. FRANKLIN SMITH,
No. 327 Walnut Street, P. O. Box 2423 Philadelphia, Pa.

Max Rosenthal, L. Franklin Smith, Philadelphia, 1863. Library of Congress, Alfred Whital Stern Collection of Lincolniana.

There were serious attempts early on to capture Lincoln as Emancipator. A portrait by Philadelphia artist Edward D. Marchant depicted the symbolic chains of slavery broken, and it inspired a campaign print for the 1864 election. For the most part, though, 1864 campaign images were rather silent where emancipation was concerned.

Ehrgott, Forbriger & Co., 1863, after a painting by David Gilmour Blythe.
Library of Congress Prints and Photographs Division.

The pictorial enterprises that dealt with emancipation were
mostly unsuccessful. A composition by David Gilmour Blythe
was cluttered with symbols, like the Bible Lincoln holds in his
lap to inspire the Proclamation. The Blythe painting, too,
inspired a print adaptation (above), but not a familiar one,
because it was not popular. As a result, there are not many
copies remaining.

An anti-emancipation tradition co-existed with the emancipation imagery in the early visual literature. In an etching by
Adalbert Volck, the Bible was again featured, but Lincoln was
stomping it with his foot as he wrote words in ink that came
right out of Satan's inkwell (page 83, top). In a cartoon from the
Southern Illustrated News, a periodical struggling to remain alive in
Richmond, Lincoln was unmasked not as an Emancipator but as
the devil himself (page 83, bottom). The cartoon featured a
gallows made of Lincolnian rails, erected for Lincoln in the dis-
tance on the unfinished stump of the Washington Monument.
In the view of anti-Republican image-makers during the 1864
campaign, emancipation would lead inexorably to a society that
embraced miscegenation, as illustrated by G. W. Bromley & Co.

Adalbert J. Volck, Baltimore, 1863. Library of Congress Prints and Photographs Division.

King Abraham before and after issuing the EMANCIPATION PROCLAMATION.

Southern Illustrated News, Richmond, Virginia, 1863.

A.H. Ritchie, c1866, after a painting by Francis B. Carpenter. Library of Congress, Alfred Whital Stern Collection of Lincolniana.

in a famous cartoon that depicted Lincoln bowing to a mixed race couple, in a supposedly horrific scene.

The man who changed the way we view emancipation was Francis B. Carpenter, an artist from upstate New York who won a commission to work at the Executive Mansion. He spent six months there, and commissioned in the President's office, now the Lincoln Bedroom, the first photograph ever taken of a president inside the White House. Carpenter had other photographs made for this very complicated enterprise. He then produced preliminary drawings and sketched out the first reading of the Emancipation Proclamation with characters placed very carefully, including Andrew Jackson lurking in the background in a painting on the wall. Ultimately, Carpenter created the heroic painting currently on view in the U.S. Capitol, hanging above the staircase outside the Senate Gallery.

The immediate impact of the Carpenter painting was magnified by the announcement that it would be made into an engraving. Lincoln signed on as the first subscriber. The resulting print proved immensely popular, becoming what was probably the best selling image of the entire nineteenth century (above). While it may look unremarkable to us today—just a group of white guys sitting around holding papers—it crystallized for white audiences of its day a truly historic event, and did so without the inconvenience and commercial risk of portraying black people.

One of the pieces of evidence we can use to measure a print's popularity is the number of copies it inspired from competitors. Carpenter was copied by many rival printmakers, who ripped him off with impunity because there were no enforceable copyright laws. In one imitation, New York engraver Edward Herline juggled the positions of the cabinet members, who were arranged meaningfully in the original, with liberals on the left and conservatives on the right. Herline just wanted to make his version a little different. So did another printmaker from New York, Thomas Kelly, who brought General Grant into the scene (below) to convert it into a generic cabinet meeting.

While the printers were mostly based in the northern cities of New York, Boston, and Philadelphia, they were eager to sell prints on the newly re-opened southern market. Kelly's next version, the ultimate piracy of the Carpenter original, pictured

T. Kelly, New York. Library of Congress Prints and Photographs Division.

PRESIDENT LINCOLN AND HIS CABINET.

T. Kelly, New York. Library of Congress Prints and Photographs Division.

Jefferson Davis and his cabinet with Robert E. Lee (above). Lost on southern audiences was the fact that it took place in the White House. Particularly lost was the fact that Jefferson Davis was holding the Emancipation Proclamation.

There were other emancipation prints by this time, including Thomas Nast's conception of an African-American family hearing the news of the emancipation above a large medallion portrait tribute to Lincoln (page 87, top).

Then something interesting happened. Frederick Douglass promoted a portrait of Hiram Revels, the first African American elected to the U.S. Senate, to a seat once held by Jefferson Davis. Douglass declared, "Heretofore colored Americans have thought little of adorning their parlors. Pictures come not with slavery and oppression, but with liberty, fair play, leisure, and refinement. The walls of their homes will soon begin to bear evidence of their altered relations to the people about them."

So audiences began to see prints made for the black marketplace. It is true that they were made by white entrepreneurs, but they were made for a new, widening, and ever more diverse audience. One of my favorites (page 87, bottom) showed an "angel of color" descending from heaven to inspire Lincoln to write the Proclamation, and in case the message was not clear,

Thomas Nast, c1865. Library of Congress Prints and Photographs Division.

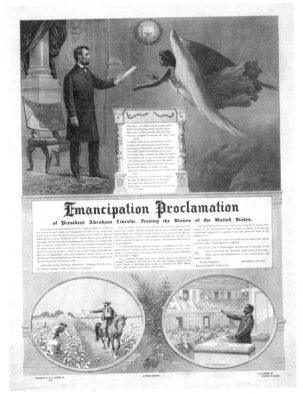

A.B. Daniel, Sr. Tuscaloosa, Alabama, 1896. Library of Congress, Alfred Whital Stern Collection of Lincolniana.

that one should buy this picture and tell family and friends and neighbors to buy it, the print included a poem:

> Reverence him though our skins are dark,
> Reverence him in our churches and park;
> Let us teach our children to do the same,
> And teach them never to forget his name.

This print once again demonstrates a commercial reaction to a changing marketplace.

Some of the images seem retrograde to modern viewers, like the motif of the kneeling, grateful slave that is apparent in some prints. Currier & Ives of New York surely knew that Lincoln had never personally liberated a slave family (below). Another print shows a dignified slave family hearing the news of emancipation from a soldier (page 89, top), while Lincoln appears only as a remote decorative portrait in the margins.

The Thomas Ball emancipation statue (page 89, bottom) was

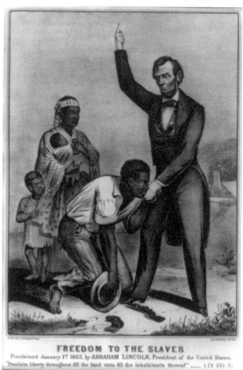

FREEDOM TO THE SLAVES
Proclaimed January 1ˢᵗ 1863, by ABRAHAM LINCOLN, President of the United States.
"Proclaim liberty throughout All the land unto All the inhabitants thereof" ..... LEV XXV 10.

Currier & Ives, New York, 1863–1870. Library of Congress Prints and Photographs Division.

J. W. Watts, 1864, after a painting by H. W. Herrick. Library of
Congress Prints and Photographs Division.

Thomas Ball, Lincoln Statue, Washington, D.C., 1876. Library of
Congress Prints and Photographs Division.

raised in Lincoln Park in the Capitol Hill neighborhood of Washington, D.C. in 1876, and Frederick Douglass gave a famous dedicatory speech. The statue has been controversial almost ever since, although it inspired postcards and other mementoes. Up through World War I, Lincoln remained a symbol in popular art designed for African-American homes. A typical print depicted an African-American veteran coming home from the Great War. The scene was set in the home, where a flag-draped Lincoln portrait was displayed on the mantel, a reflection of Lincoln's enduring popularity.

The best known monument to Lincoln, of course, is the Lincoln Memorial (page 91) in Washington D.C., finished in 1922. The dedication ceremony featured President Harding and ex-President Taft, who spoke before a crowd that was almost violently segregated by mounted police, with African Americans pushed to the back. The only African-American speaker that day was Robert Moton of the Tuskegee Institute, whose call to live up to the promise of emancipation and the Gettysburg Address was censored by the Harding administration. Moton was told, in essence, "If you don't want to do it our way, don't do it," and so he did it their way.

Moton was the only speaker of color that day, and yet over the next thirty to forty years, thanks to Marian Anderson's famous concert and the March on Washington and Martin Luther King's Dream Speech, the Lincoln Memorial emerged as the backdrop to national aspirations. This was never more true than after the election of President Obama. The two Presidents—Lincoln and Obama—have appeared together in a succession of newspaper and magazine cartoons. I was astonished in my own research by how many images exist, not just because President Obama held his pre-inaugural festivities at the Lincoln Memorial, but because the connection between them is simply irresistible.

The Obama inauguration in 2009 marked the return of the Lincoln Memorial to a pre-eminent place in the national consciousness, to a degree not seen since the Kennedy assassination and the famous Bill Mauldin cartoon of a weeping Memorial. Through it all, the image of Lincoln as a liberator has evolved and today remains something of a paradox, just as it seemed to poet Langston Hughes. Hughes encountered the Memorial in 1926, and saw Lincoln there as the heroic father figure yet also remote and maybe even indifferent.

I do not pretend that Hughes' words are conclusive in understanding, appreciating, or contradicting the complicated and changing image of Lincoln as a liberator, but they reveal that as early as 1926, and ever since, we have grappled with this changing image.

> Let's go see Old Abe
> Sitting in the marble and the moonlight
> Sitting lonely in the marble and the moonlight
> Quiet for 10,000 Centuries, old Abe
> Quiet for a million, million years
> Quiet
> And yet a voice forever
> Against the
> Timeless walls
> Of time
> Old Abe.

Marjorie Collins, 1944. Library of Congress Prints and Photographs Division.

Harriet Jacobs. Photo courtesy of Jean Fagan Yellin.

Harriet Jacobs in the Refugee Camps

Jean Fagan Yellin

I came today to talk about memory, to discuss Harriet Jacobs and the black Civil War refugees, and as the day has progressed it occurred to me that I need to explain who Harriet Jacobs was and who the Civil War refugees were.

First, let me begin by introducing Jacobs, a fugitive slave, an author, and an activist—a hero of the Civil War period. We know of two other heroic black women, Harriet Tubman and Sojourner Truth, and can read their narratives, but these are as-told-to stories because both women—illiterate by law—were unable to write. Until very recently, we have not remembered Harriet Jacobs, my subject this afternoon. Unlike Tubman and Truth, Harriet Jacobs was literate, and she wrote her own story.

Second, I will talk about the black Civil War refugees. Growing up in Michigan, all I ever knew of Civil War refugees were those wonderful old photographs of emaciated white people standing in front of chimneys, all that remained of their burned out mansions. It never occurred to me that there were black Civil War refugees. But there were—thousands and thousands of them. Finally, I will comment briefly about American memory.

Let me introduce Harriet Jacobs. She was born in Edenton,

North Carolina on Albemarle Sound in 1813 to Delilah and
Elijah Jacobs. Like her mother, she was owned by the
Horniblow family. Her mother died when Harriet was six, and
her young mistress took charge of her and taught her to read.
Then when Harriet was twelve, the mistress died. In her will is
an unsigned codicil written the day of her death. It declares that
she is willing "my Negro girl, Harriet, and my bureau and work
table and its contents" to her little niece. This meant that twelve-
year-old Harriet (along with a sewing table) was moved into the
home of a three-year-old, whose father proved to be a lecher. In
her teens, Harriet suffered endless sexual harassment. In order
to end it, she became sexually involved with a prominent
neighbor (who was more influential than her owner, hence
perhaps able to protect her), and by him she had two children.
But the harassment continued. When she was twenty-one, her
master threatened that if she would not bow to his sexual
demands, he would send her children out to the plantation to
become plantation slaves.

Harriet was a town woman. She had never worked on the
plantation, but she knew what it would mean if her children
were sent to be plantation slaves. She certainly knew what it
would mean for her young daughter. She decided she had to
save them, but the question was, how? Her answer was to run
off, reasoning that if she were gone, her master would not want
to be bothered with the children, and that their father would buy
and free them. Harriet ran, and her master advertised her escape
and issued a wanted ad: "Hundred dollar reward will be given
for the apprehension and delivery of my servant girl, Harriet."
The description, as written by the man who had lusted after her
since she was twelve, reads:

> She is a light mulatto 21 years of age, about five feet four
> inches high, of a thick and corpulent habit, having on her
> head a thick covering of black hair and curling naturally but
> which can easily be combed straight. She speaks easily and
> fluently and has an agreeable carriage and address. Being a
> good seamstress, she has been accustomed to dress well,
> has a variety of very fine clothes made in the prevailing
> fashion and will probably appear, if abroad, tricked out and
> gay in fashionable finery.

Now a fugitive, she briefly—and dangerously—hid with sympathetic neighbors in town. It was impossible for her to leave because the roads and sea-lanes on the Albemarle were patrolled. Next to Edenton is a huge swamp, part of the Great Dismal Swamp. She had nowhere to go. Ultimately, she hid in the attic of her grandmother's home. Her grandmother, by this time a freed woman, was Edenton's baker. In her attic, a hiding place was built for Harriet. A floor plan of the grandmother's house shows a cross-section of the porch and the attic above it. Here Harriet hid for six years and eleven months. Twenty years ago, readers found this unbelievable. I did not believe it, but I was able to find documentation. I found the wanted ad dated June 30, 1835, and a letter describing her escape dated June 25, 1842, written just as she went north from Philadelphia to New York. She was indeed in that attic for six years and eleven months.

Harriet finally arrived in New York. She found her brother and heard the story of his escape; she got her children to the North (two more stories); she became involved with the abolitionists; and her freedom was bought. When free, she wrote, "Since I have no fear of my name coming before those whom I have lived in dread of, I cannot be happy without trying to be useful in some way." By "useful" she meant useful to the movement, useful to freedom. Her way of becoming useful was to write her gripping story, which she was finally was able to publish in 1861, and then the next year in England.

The title page of her book is strange. She wrote pseudonymously as "Linda Brent," a nineteenth-century woman telling the story of her sexual harassment and of her struggle against it. She certainly could not use her own name, as she believed her story was too shameful to tell in public. The title page reads "Incidents in the Life of a Slave Girl Written by Herself, Edited by L. Maria Child." Lydia Maria Child was a well known abolitionist author, and it makes sense that Child would have edited a slave narrative. The page also announces, "Published for the author, 1861." For librarians, this presents a problem. This book has no author and no publisher. It was cataloged in the Library of Congress under "Linda Brent, pseudonym." Now authenticated and republished, Harriet Jacobs' book is listed under her own name. The story she tells of her struggle against sexual exploitation in slavery certainly is some of the tough stuff of American history.

In the North, Harriet Jacobs allied herself with the abolitionists who were eager to transform the Civil War into a war for freedom, as was the black population of this country as a whole. On December 8, 1862, anticipating emancipation, which Lincoln had announced six months earlier, Jacobs wrote, "The last six months has been the happiest of all my life. I guess God is settling the account." With the onset of the Civil War, she decided that she should come back south and aid the refugees seeking freedom behind the Union lines.

Concerning the black Civil War refugees: growing up where and when I did, I certainly had never heard of any such. Studying the documents, I learned that entire families of people who had been held in slavery on plantations near federal encampments escaped to the Union Army. Harriet Jacobs worked for a brief time with the refugees crowding the federal capital, then went to Alexandria, Virginia, behind the Union lines. Alexandria, which had been a hub of the slave trade, became a center for black refugees from slavery. Here Harriet Jacobs worked with the contrabands—fugitives from slavery—helping them obtain food and medical care, and arranging for clothing and money to be sent to them from people and relief organizations in the North. Contraband women in the camps often worked as cooks and laundry women; contraband men worked for the Union Army; and a great many contraband orphaned children were on their own.

Working with the black refugees in the camp at Alexandria, Jacobs transformed herself into a war correspondent. She wrote to the northern press, telling of the distress she witnessed every day. Overwhelmed by their need, in a private letter she exclaimed, "If ever I craved more than one pair of hands and money it's now. The good God has spared me for this." To the press, she reported, "The misery I've witnessed must be seen to be believed. Very many in Alexandria [have] died from destitution. It's impossible to reach them all [with aid]. Government has erected here barracks for the accommodation of 500. We have 1,500 on the list." In her newspaper pieces, Jacobs urged her readers to assume an attitude different from that of many of the other correspondents in the South who despised the contrabands. Instead, she wrote, "Trust them, make them free, give them the responsibility of caring for themselves. Some of them know little else than the handle of the plow, the cotton pad, and the overseer's lash. You will find them as apt to learn as any other people that come to you, stupid from oppression."

Jacobs hailed the decision to permit black troops to join the Union Army. She felt, when she saw black men in their blue uniforms, that the United States was finally her country. Her work with the refugees was difficult, but the freed people were, she believed, becoming successful in making the transition from slaves into freed men and women. Later, however—after the war had ended, while she was doing relief work in Savannah—the planters regained the land that had been set aside for the freed people. The former slaves were forced to sign contracts with their old masters, contracts that placed them not back into slavery, but into another version of servitude. If they protested and organized, they were threatened by visits from the Ku Klux Klan. In July of 1865, in the face of the dispossession of the land and the growing anti-black violence, Jacobs wrote, "Be not discouraged. Deeds of mercy moveth even the heart of a man who may hate his Brother. We must march on though with but a broken lance, though we have no lance at all." The following year, after the murder of a colleague who was, like her, connected with the New England Freedmen's Aid Society, Harriet Jacobs retreated to the North.

And what of our national memory? To talk about Harriet Jacobs and her work, and to talk about the black Civil War refugees, is to talk about American memory—about what we as a nation have chosen to remember, and about what we have chosen to forget. Today, few know of this courageous woman or of these black refugees. But Jacobs's story, and the stories of the transitions of a people from slavery to freedom, and then to a system of segregation, are the "tough stuff" of American history. They are American stories. We need to freshen our memories.

Addressing the Causes of the Civil War in Public History

Dwight T. Pitcaithley

I have been asked to talk about the public discussion involving the causes of the Civil War, how it plays out, how those arguments are made, and how history is told and retold in the public arena. There is a different rhythm to the popular discussion we have about the causes of the war than we have in academic circles. Jim Horton told me years ago that if I proposed a session to the Organization of American Historians about whether slavery was a cause of the Civil War it would probably not make it onto the program, because that has been pretty much settled in scholarly circles for a number of decades, thanks to many of the people who have spoken today.

In the public sector it is a different story. I was teaching in Tennessee about four years ago, talking to a young man about the Civil War, and it came about that I was teaching the Civil War at Middle Tennessee State. He asked, "I hope you are teaching the true history of the war."

I responded that I was, but I wondered: what did he mean?

He answered, "Well, you know it wasn't about slavery, because most southerners didn't own slaves." As far as he was concerned, that was the end of the story. There was no negotiation or conversation about the causes of the war at all. It

was about states' rights, of course, and not slavery, and he and
others who are convinced of that have come by that position
honestly. There is an old tradition, the "Lost Cause"
interpretation of the war, which has been referenced several
times today. Alexander Stephens and Jefferson Davis probably
began this interpretation with their histories of the war,
supported a little later by Jubal Early's, all of which made the
same point—that the war was really about states' rights. Slavery
was simply incidental to the run-up of the war. The idea that the
war was not about slavery was then carried on by the children of
Confederates in the form of the United Daughters of the
Confederacy and the Sons of Confederate Veterans.

One of my favorite historians was a grand promoter of the
Lost Cause interpretation: Mildred Lewis Rutherford. She held
the title Historian General of the United Daughters of the
Confederacy, and she took her job very seriously. She published
widely. Many of her records and scrapbooks are in Richmond at
the Museum of the Confederacy. She wrote a number of books
with titles like *The South Must Have Her Rightful Place in History*,
from 1923. My favorite is *Truths of History: A Fair, Unbiased,
Impartial, Unprejudiced, and Conscientious Study of History. Object: To
Secure a Peaceful Settlement of the Many Perplexing Questions Now
Causing Contention Between the North and the South*, published in
1920.

All her books revolved around a couple of themes that
portrayed a sentimental version of the antebellum South,
bolstered the white supremacy convictions of her generation,
and presented, of course, the true cause of secession. *Truths of
History* is still in print—there is a 1998 edition with a glowing
introduction. Rutherford set the pattern for subsequent books
on the Lost Cause by organizing her chapters along statements
such as "Secession was not rebellion," "The North was
responsible for the War Between the States," "The South was
more interested in the freedom of the slaves than the North,"
and "The War Between the States was not fought to hold
slaves." Under each chapter heading, she would include a series
of quotes, taken completely out of context and not necessarily

arranged in any order, to make whatever point the chapter heading suggested. That rhythm has been followed in a number of current books that are on the market at your local bookstore.

The Lost Cause interpretation stays current in spite of a large body of scholarship. As my bicycling partner in Las Cruces, who is a European scholar, wondered, "Why doesn't it stay lost?" But it does not. The Lost Cause remains alive and well. The National Park Service confronted that interpretation in 1998, when a number of superintendents and National Park Service employees of Civil War battlefields met in Nashville to consider some issues related to general battlefield management, including the interpretation of the battlefields. The attendees decided unanimously that 1998 was a good time to start talking about the causes of the war. It had been an unwritten policy since 1933, when the Civil War battlefields were inherited from the Department of War, that the Park Service did not talk about causes. The causes were too complex, too contentious, and the Park Service did not want to rile the public.

In Virginia during the 1930s, that concern played out in an interesting way. A number of Civil War battlefields were and are in Virginia, and the National Park Service developed a deal with the state government that it would not produce any interpretive product, pamphlet, or exhibit without getting the approval of the state historian and of Douglas Southall Freeman. The National Park Service wanted to ensure that it did not say anything "obnoxious" about the South or about slavery.

When the decisions of the 1998 meeting became public, the National Park Service received about 2,200 cards and letters, mostly as a result of write-in campaigns by the Sons of Confederate Veterans and Civil War Roundtables. These letters asked the director to overturn the decision of the superintendents, to stop being "politically correct," and to return to the earlier policy of not interpreting causes. Because I held the position of chief historian of the National Park Service, all those 2,200 cards and letters ended up on my desk. The letter writers, or taxpayers, after all, had a right to know what the Park Service was doing and why. I thought, this will be easy; I had read *Battle Cry of Freedom*. I would quote Jim McPherson.

Well, it turns out that, according to those who raised the complaint, in spite of his Pulitzer Prize, Jim is just a "Yankee historian," and he really does not know much about southern history. So I tried citing some southern historians, and it turns out they were considered "scalawag historians." So that did not get me anywhere either. The National Park Service learned a lot of lessons from this experience. One of them is that the more you can base your arguments or your presentations on original sources, the better off you are going to be. This is advice Jim Horton gave me years ago, and it certainly has stood us in good stead.

We found essentially neutral ground by talking about and using the words of the secessionists themselves. Four states developed declarations of secession. These were formal statements that were designed to inform people exactly why secession was necessary. South Carolina, Georgia, Mississippi, and Texas all developed such declarations. Mississippi's begins, "Our position is thoroughly identified with the institution of slavery—the greatest material interest in the world." The rest of the paragraph goes on to explain why a threat to slavery was a threat to southern commerce and to southern civilization. When the first tier of southern states seceded, they appointed commissioners to visit other slave states to convince them to secede as well. We can read the commissioners' arguments, letters, and speeches and get a fine sense, a very clear sense, of what the war was all about. We know much about this thanks to Charles Dew, who wrote a book a few years ago about the secession commissioners, titled *Apostles of Disunion*.

Finally, we used several compromise proposals. Every textbook presents the story of John J. Crittenden, Senator from Kentucky, and his set of five compromise proposals that were designed as an amendment to the Constitution to solve the problem of secession. All five dealt with protecting slavery: in the territories, in Washington, D.C., bolstering the Fugitive Slave Act, allowing the transportation of slaves, and protecting slavery at federal installations in the South. Crittenden's sixth article stipulated that all these amendments would be unamendable. If Congress had passed Crittenden's suggestion and the states had ratified it, slavery would have been embedded in the Constitution in perpetuity.

What I know now that I did not know ten years ago is that there is a vast and deep collection of primary sources waiting to be explored, in the form of the state secession convention journals. Eleven states called secession conventions and they all kept meticulous records. They elected delegates and officers, and recorded all the votes, proposals, and suggestions for compromise. With the exception of Texas, every state published them during 1861 or 1862. Texas waited until 1912, claiming it did not have money until then. What we find in the journals are the original arguments in favor of secession because Lincoln was an abolitionist and because the Republican Party was an abolitionist party. We need to leave, secessionists argued, to protect the institution of slavery.

From Alabama, we find G. T. Yelverton saying, "The question of slavery is the rock upon which the old government split. It is the cause of secession." John T. Morgan, also from Alabama, observed, "The ordinance of secession rests in great measure upon our assertion of the right to enslave the African race, or what amounts to the same thing, to hold them in slavery."

Virginia deliberated the longest of any state, and produced the longest record—four volumes, almost three thousand pages. Thomas Goode, who represented Mecklenburg County, pronounced, "The great question which is now uprooting this government to its foundation, the great question which underlies all our deliberations here is the question of African slavery."

As this nation begins its remembrance of the Civil War at the 150-year mark, it is my hope that collectively we can regain our curiosity about the war and its causes. Instead of relying on tired bromides regarding the war's origins—bromides widely repeated North and South—how refreshing it would be to have a public conversation based on the words of the secessionists themselves. Here in Virginia, for example, we could have a conversation about secession based on the official and published four-volume record of the state's secession convention, which can now be found online (see Further Reading, page 133).

The stakes are high. Until we have a clear and accurate understanding of the causes of secession, we cannot appreciate the meaning and legacy of the war. And there is no better way to start a public exchange of views on the subject during this first year of the Sesquicentennial than by reflecting upon the hopes and fears of the secessionists as recorded in the journals of the eleven state secession conventions.

PANEL II DISCUSSION

Panel II: James O. Horton, David Blight, Jean Fagan Yellin, Harold Holzer, James McPherson, and Dwight T. Pitcaithley.

JAMES HORTON I just want to add a few things about the difficulty that you face sometimes when you talk about the significance of slavery in the coming of the Civil War. During the early 1990s, the Park Service superintendent at Gettysburg gave a lecture at the Department of the Interior. He talked about slavery as one of the important causes of the Civil War. He did not talk about it as the only cause. More than a thousand people wrote letters to the Secretary of the Interior demanding that this superintendent be fired because, they argued, he knew nothing about the Civil War. So, if you are providing history to the general public and you talk about slavery as one of the significant causes of the Civil War, you may face real trouble.

In the late 1990s I did an interview on television and I talked about slavery and the coming of the Civil War. A few days later, I got a letter from a schoolteacher in Houston, Texas. She was new to the area and had not been there long enough to have tenure. In her classroom in a public school, she talked about slavery as one of the important causes of the Civil War. The parents of her students did not want their children to learn this about the Civil War because, they argued, it was not true. So they organized and put pressure on the principal of the school to fire the teacher.

If you talk about slavery and the Civil War, you really have to present evidence that is difficult to refute. This is one of the important issues that we need to deal with as we go through the period of the Civil War Sesquicentennial.

DAVID BLIGHT That is why we told these stories. I am the last to be the Pollyanna on any subject, but that is why Jim McPherson tells us about the scale of the escape to the Union Navy. That is why Harold stresses the imagery of emancipation as it changes over time, and why Jean tells us about Harriet Jacobs' role in those contraband camps, and so on. I am all for knowing where the problem is, but sometimes we just have to answer Mildred Rutherford, as Dwight so nicely pointed out, by throwing the other stories back at her and at anyone who still wants to admire Ms. Mildred, as she was called in Athens, Georgia. It is stories against stories. It is just that some stories are truer than others.

HAROLD HOLZER I would like to turn the focus back to Lincoln for a couple of comments. The generation after Ms. Mildred, or "General Mildred," is the generation of "new" historians, among them Thomas DiLorenzo, who assert that Lincoln actually coalesced federal power to such a degree that he created the permanent welfare state, big government, America as dictatorial policeman of the world, and all the other ills and perceived ills that come from federalism and the reverse of states' rights. It is part of the same rewriting of history mindset.

Even as we accept that we have to debate and correct these undocumented views, it is still important to remember that, as we talk about the slow march to freedom and the pain of people who were denied freedom for so long, the Emancipation Proclamation at the time of its issuance was deeply controversial and evoked a huge degree of opposition. This was manifested in ways that Lincoln himself witnessed: a decline in the stock market and increased desertion among the troops. Certainly he was warned in his own cabinet that his party would be defeated in the 1862 midterm elections, and that is sort of an analogy to what we face in our own midterm elections in 2010. Lincoln was warned by his postmaster general that the Republican Party, the administration, would be decisively defeated if he issued a proclamation before the midterm elections in 1862, which he did anyway. It was a deeply controversial thing, opposed not just in the South among people who were used to slavery and had an economic interest in slavery, but in the North among Democrats who did not count themselves as abolitionists.

We need to remember, too, that abolitionism was a radical political movement. Charles Leland of Philadelphia, the fellow who was responsible for one of the printed versions of the Emancipation Proclamation, claimed in his memoir to be the person who found the path to a greater acceptance of freedom by replacing the word "abolition" with "emancipation" in the national vocabulary. I have no idea if he deserves credit, but he certainly took credit.

DWIGHT PITCAITHLEY Emancipation, of course, is the thread that runs through our conversation here. We are all aware that in any town in the South and in many in the North you will find Civil War monuments, statues, and so forth. We passed an obelisk to the Confederacy on our way here from the hotel. Every square has them. We even have them in New Mexico. Highway I-10 through New Mexico is the Jefferson Davis Highway, with markers along the way. But where are the emancipation monuments and statues? Harold showed the Thomas Ball statue (page 89), which I think is properly categorized as a Lincoln statue, although it was supposed to be an emancipation statue. The Emancipation Proclamation, or part of it, is on the front.

Where is the national monument to emancipation, clearly the most single significant outcome of the war? I would like to think that one of the outcomes of the Sesquicentennial nationally would be the development of a national emancipation monument in Washington, D.C.

HAROLD HOLZER It is a very good question. There is

currently a movement in Washington for an emancipation monument. There is a timeline, an iconographical change that you can see if you check the dates of Lincoln sculpture, monumental sculpture, and public sculpture. From 1876 when the Ball statue was unveiled in Washington through about World War I, almost all of the sculpture was emancipation driven. And then with the inconvenience of the fact that we did not complete the unfinished work, things became much more generic, and there are many more sculptures of Lincoln the orator or the grand Lincoln, as in the Lincoln Memorial.

The most brutal reminder that emancipation was driven out of the Lincoln memory comes in the inscribed words in the Lincoln Memorial, which you, the taxpayer, through the Bicentennial Commission, paid to have re-etched so we could read it more easily. I will not even tell you how much that cost the taxpayers, just for the ink. The Gettysburg Address is inscribed there, along with his second inaugural, brilliant speeches to be sure, but emancipation is nowhere in that monument.

JAMES McPHERSON It seems to me that the second inaugural is all about the emancipation, so I am not sure that I would quite go along with that.

DAVID BLIGHT "Every drop of blood shed."

HAROLD HOLZER Yes, it is all about slavery and freedom.

JAMES McPHERSON "Judge not, that ye be not judged," and so on.

HAROLD HOLZER Lincoln imperiled the reputation of emancipation and his reputation as a liberator by insisting on writing the Proclamation in legalistic and not philanthropic prose.

JAMES McPHERSON Sure—that was in 1863. But by 1865 it was a different story, with the second inaugural address. I mean, in some ways that is the most eloquent of all Lincoln speeches with respect to slavery as not only a cause of the war, which he explicitly said, but emancipation as the great result, really ordained by God. This is a sermon in which he said that maybe the war was a punishment for three centuries of slavery.

JEAN FAGAN YELLIN To return to the stories, over the last fifteen or twenty years, I have heard people say again and again that there are no sources. We can't do the history of African Americans or of women or whomever, because there are no sources and so it is all just imaginary, and we are very sorry but we have to leave that out. What David has shown today with the John Washington material and what I found with the Jacobs material is that, yes, of course, there are sources. They are not in the textbooks.

These sources may be included when the next textbook is written. And ordinary people can do research, not just fancy Ph.D. historians. Often our students have aunts who have papers in the attic, and I am convinced that if we would all go and clean out the attics we would have many, many more stories to tell about African Americans and about women.

DAVID BLIGHT The John Washington story is a box in the attic story that came down through his family. I would like to add a word about the monuments. The greatest work of art about the Civil War (and I feel sure the art historians would agree) is the Shaw Memorial by Augustus Saint-Gaudens in Boston. I happen to think it is also the most meaningful monument, and certainly the most moving to me. Ask yourself when you go to any Civil War monument: Does it move you? Which ones do? Usually it is because you are invested in the story. Even the most nondescript generic memorial may be meaningful if, for example, your great-grandfather was in the regiment depicted.

With the Shaw Memorial, Saint Gaudens acknowledges as men those black Union soldiers marching to their deaths. It is a magical work of art. Now, why there are not a thousand other such monuments is a great question. Why are Civil War sites not emancipation sites?

DWIGHT PITCAITHLEY I am reminded of an emancipation statue called "The Freed Slave," by Francesco Pizzicar, that was displayed at the Centennial Exposition in Philadelphia in

1876. William Dean Howells, an author of the period, found the figure of the man emerging from broken chains aesthetically uninspiring, and famously remarked that it made him want to "clap him back into hopeless slavery." As it turns out, that statue was not kept in the United States, but is now in a museum in Trieste, Italy.

In the collection at Howard University there is a smaller emancipation statue called "Forever Free," by an African-American woman, Edmonia Lewis. These are smaller versions of potentially larger pieces of sculpture, but larger versions were never made because the emphasis changed.

HAROLD HOLZER You know, it is an artistic challenge. It is a tough thing to do. The early pieces of Lincoln sculpture simply showed a tall figure clutching a document. Sometimes the word "emancipation" was included on the sculpture or at the base.

This year, at the Soldiers and Sailors Monument in Cleveland, I saw a terrific piece, a bronze bas-relief panel like the Shaw. This panel, by Lewis Scofield, depicts Lincoln and a liberated slave, not lifting a slave to freedom, no shackles, but handing a rifle to the liberated slave. I would like to see more attention given to that piece. I think it is absolutely unique in Lincoln public art.

DAVID BLIGHT That changes the story, does it not?

HAROLD HOLZER Well, it was 1880.

JAMES HORTON One of the things we saw this morning was a picture of a statue of Lincoln with a slave kneeling in front of him (page 89). That statue is on Capitol Hill in Washington, D.C. The slave is kneeling there and Lincoln has in his hand the Emancipation Proclamation. The interesting thing about that statue is that it is the result of a relationship between Abraham Lincoln and Frederick Douglass. That statue was put up in 1876, and Frederick Douglass gave the speech as the statue was unveiled. In it he talked about his relationship with Lincoln, saying to the white people in the audience, "you are his children," and, referring to black people, "we are his stepchildren." He went on to tell how his relationship with Lincoln helped him psychologically. What kind of relationship did this former slave have with the President of the United States? They first met when Frederick Douglass went to the White House to talk to Lincoln about the discrepancy in pay between black soldiers and white soldiers in the Union Army. Black soldiers got roughly half of what white soldiers got, and Douglass went to talk to Lincoln to see if he could change the situation. When Douglass went to the White House, Lincoln greeted him, shook his hand, and said, "Oh, you are Frederick Douglass. I have heard of you." They sat and talked, and finally Lincoln agreed that yes, something should be done to make the pay more equitable. That was in the early 1860s, just after the war had started.

Lincoln invited Frederick Douglass to his second inaugural address in 1865. There was a party afterward at the White House, and at first the guard did not let Douglass in. One of the people at the door said, "This is a friend of the President," so the guard let him in. When Frederick Douglass walked in, Lincoln said to him, in front of all the people, "I am so glad you are here. I want to ask you what you thought of my inauguration, my inaugural address." He then added, "You know, I have more respect for your opinion than anybody I can think of." Can you imagine this in 1865, at a party in the White House? Lincoln walks up and shakes Douglass' hand, and he acts like, yeah, this is a good friend of mine.

This story gives you some sense of Abraham Lincoln and what happened to him as the Civil War moved along, as he set up the Emancipation Proclamation. The second inaugural address was much different than the first, in which he said that he would not interfere with the institution of slavery in places where it currently existed, but that he did not want it to expand. His second inaugural address was much more anti-slavery.

HAROLD HOLZER One thing on the relationship between Lincoln and Douglass: a test of that relationship, and it could have been an important test because Lincoln fully expected to lose the election, came when Lincoln and Douglass conferred in the White House and devised an impractical but sincere plan to spread the news of the Emancipation Proclamation in the South. This was to be done through an army of African-American bounty hunters, who would be rewarded for each person they notified. They would spread the news of the Proclamation where there were advancing armies or, as Jim McPherson reminds us, where the Union Navy was making inroads.

They had to get the news out, because if McClellan was elected President he would rescind the order. Douglass wrote a plan of action, which was never acted on, but it is a fascinating example of two great minds coming together and trying to clear the way for that step toward freedom.

DAVID BLIGHT   We have to be a little careful about these primary documents, because the story of that third meeting between Douglass and Lincoln, though deeply moving, is based on one solitary paragraph in Frederick Douglass' autobiography. Douglass is the only source we have of that story.

JAMES HORTON   There is other documentation of that friendship. After Lincoln was assassinated, Douglass received a letter from Lincoln's wife, saying that Lincoln would have wanted him to have his walking cane. Douglass wrote back saying that he would love to have it. Douglass' home in Maryland is now a National Park Service site, and in the study of that house you can see Douglass' collection of walking canes, including the one from Lincoln.

HAROLD HOLZER   She gave another cane to Francis Carpenter, the artist who painted the first reading of the Emancipation Proclamation. There seems to be a theme there.

DAVID BLIGHT   Jean used an important word in her presentation: refugees. This massive total war, if that is a fair phrase, produced hundreds of thousands of refugees, huge numbers of which had been slaves. It was a revolutionary process that made the historical circumstances of black freedom possible. The emancipation was not a day. It was not a singing jubilee, although people did sing. It was hundreds of thousands of moments, many of them in terror and under tremendous hardship. Hundreds of people, if not thousands, died in the contraband camps where Harriet Jacobs worked. At one point Jacobs wrote that ten to fifteen people were dying every day.

JEAN FAGAN YELLIN Every morning she came to see how many had died since the previous day. There was a room covered with lime where they put the bodies.

DAVID BLIGHT They were burying the dead every day. People were drowning while trying to get to the Union Navy. It is a story of tremendous turmoil, hardship, suffering, as well as celebration. That just needs to be said.

JEAN FAGAN YELLIN You know, in this country we are accustomed to refugees from other countries, but these refugees were our own people. A more recent example of that was Hurricane Katrina, where suddenly there were American refugees, and it was a serious issue for the country.

JAMES HORTON I would like to point out two quick things. In 2005 there was an exhibit at the New York Historical Society called "Slavery in New York." I was the chief historian for that exhibit and I want to tell you that there were lots of people who were surprised and some who were upset by the exhibit, because they did not believe and did not know that there ever was slavery in New York. History can raise all kinds of objections from people who who are surprised or dismayed by what they learn.

Before the New York exhibit, a number of us did a conference in Boston about slavery in various parts of New England. During one of the breaks in the conference, I went across the street to a historic cemetery and wandered around and looked at the names of the people on the gravestones, like Paul Revere, all kinds of people.

A stranger came up to me because he saw the words "Slavery and the Slave Trade in New England" on my conference folder. He was really shocked, and he declared that

he did not believe there had been slavery or the slave trade
anywhere in New England. I assured him that there had
indeed been slavery in New England and that the slave trade
had been really important. He looked at me and said, "In New
England, maybe, but not in Boston."

I explained that, yes, Boston was a slave trading area, and
lots of slaves came into the Boston port, and lots of people
in Boston made big money on trading those slaves. He was
still shocked. The reactions I witnessed of people in New
York and Boston give a good indication that this issue of
slavery, whether it is related to the Civil War or not, is a
delicate issue in much, perhaps most, of America.

PANEL II
QUESTION & ANSWER SESSION

Moderator: William Alexander, Professor of History at Norfolk State University. Panel II: James O. Horton, David Blight, Jean Fagan Yellin, Harold Holzer, James McPherson, and Dwight T. Pitcaithley. Questions were submitted by audience members and live bloggers and via Twitter, Facebook, and email.

WILLIAM ALEXANDER This is a general question, but it has to do with perception and memory. Is there a marked difference in how slavery in the Civil War is remembered by race and age? What are the implications of the stereotype that African Americans in general do not have a strong interest in the Civil War? How do we expand and present the emancipation story inclusively in a public history way? Dwight, do you want to start?

DWIGHT PITCAITHLEY Based on my experience, one observation might be that slavery is an issue that a lot of people, black and white, do not like to talk about in public space for different reasons. We ought to talk about it more, not less, so we can better understand how it shaped this country.

HAROLD HOLZER I have a tremendous fear that memory is evaporating and that young people do not have the elementary school information that leads them to be interested in high school or college courses. I worry about this on all levels of education, all subjects. I think there is an age difference in interest in discussing and having debates, and the question is basic education.

DAVID BLIGHT Let's be honest. There has been historically a racial separation in levels of interest and in subjects of interest about this event between whites and blacks. Why have African Americans not gone to Civil War battlefield sites? With the greatest respect for my National Park Service colleagues, it is because the battlefield sites were almost entirely about a story of blue and gray, with lots of Confederate flags. African Americans historically have not attended, because until recently there were no stories about black soldiers. There are now.

We have had in this country for many years a segregated memory of this event. African-American people have commemorated a different story, by and large. Just look at the 1913 Blue/Gray Reunion at Gettysburg, the most public, symbolic moment you can imagine, the 50th anniversary of the Battle of Gettysburg. It was an entirely Jim Crow event. There were no black soldiers, no black veterans in attendance. The only black people at the Blue/Gray Reunion were the men who built the latrines, passed out blankets to the old veterans, and cooked in the mess tents. If you went to that event in 1913, you would not know that there were any black people who participated in the Civil War.

The 100th anniversary, too, was an essentially segregated story, although Bud Robertson and his colleagues improved it during the second and third years of the Centennial. To a degree we still struggle with that problem in public memory.

JEAN FAGAN YELLIN David, we are told over and over that people in my generation have much more rigid ideas about race than people in my grandchildren's generation. They may be more ignorant of the history, but their attitudes may be different too.

DAVID BLIGHT I hope so. I hope they are post-racial as they are described. Their parents and grandparents are not post-racial. Maybe the kids will convince their parents and grandparents. Boy, that is another debate. I don't know.

WILLIAM ALEXANDER Jean, is Harriet Tubman's role in the

Civil War accurately remembered in the area of public history?

JEAN FAGAN YELLIN Harriet Tubman is a very tough case because there are versions of her slave narrative written at different times, transcribed by different people, and so it is hard to know. There are three new books about Tubman coming out now.

JAMES HORTON Lois, my wife, is just finishing a manuscript on Harriet Tubman, which is part of the reason she is not here. One interesting story about Harriet Tubman is that during the war for a period of time she was the leader of some of the black Union troops.

JEAN FAGAN YELLIN Tubman really has become a mythical figure, and certainly in black history and in black culture she is all by herself. The accounting of the number of times Tubman went back South to save people changes all the time, because nobody really knows. She is sort of a shadowy heroine. I am sure Lois's book will straighten everything out.

JAMES McPHERSON A few years ago there were three books on Harriet Tubman, serious biographies by serious scholars, that came out within months of each other.

JEAN FAGAN YELLIN And for Sojourner Truth, the same is probably true.

JAMES McPHERSON At the same time there was an article by a former graduate student at Princeton who for years has taught at the University of Buffalo. He surveyed the people who were mentioned most prominently in textbooks for elementary and junior high school students, and Harriet Tubman came out near the top.

JEAN FAGAN YELLIN Really?

JAMES McPHERSON Yes, children are learning a lot about Harriet Tubman. Now, as you say, she has become something of a mythical figure and some of what they are learning is the myth of Harriet Tubman.

JEAN FAGAN YELLIN She is the Moses of her people. You cannot get better than that.

DAVID BLIGHT She is a ubiquitous subject of children's literature, which I am sure many of you know. There are more Harriet Tubman books in children's literature than you can count. So it is worth asking why.

JEAN FAGAN YELLIN With all of the millions of American women who were held in slavery, why do we know the names of only two, Sojourner Truth and Harriet Tubman? It makes no sense, except in terms of the way we have constructed our history.

DAVID BLIGHT Well, we love Harriet Tubman because every kid can imagine being an abolitionist. The Harriet Tubman story is all about slaves getting to freedom. It is not about people actually being slaves.

JAMES HORTON Yes. But there are some other things that we ought to know about African Americans who were involved in the Civil War, and, of course, there were many. We are talking about two hundred thousand African Americans involved in the war.

My wife and I have just finished editing a book that deals with the life of William Woodlin, who was born a slave in Louisiana. His master died and willed his property to his children, so William Woodlin became the property of one of his master's children, but fortunately this master's son was opposed to slavery, and he took his slaves to the North to New York and he freed them.

William Woodlin was two years old when he became free. He grew up in New York state and when the Civil War began he went to Philadelphia to enlist in the military. A central part of the book is a diary that Woodlin kept, recording the details of his time in the military and what he was doing. He was involved in all kinds of combat, but he was also part of a military band, and he had a gun and a horn. He writes that he liked the horn better than the gun, but that the gun was better protection. It is a great story.

WILLIAM ALEXANDER Harold, we would like you to start this one. It has to do with Lincoln and the emancipation. It reads like this: Lincoln's Emancipation Proclamation had various exempting clauses and proscriptions. Runaways and contrabands seem to suggest that emancipation was a singular and local event. How do we reconcile the two? And is the Proclamation as a document intended to disrupt the southern war effort worthy of public celebration as a principled act?

HAROLD HOLZER Great series of questions, and complicated. The exempting clauses in the final Proclamation made good on Lincoln's pledge to impose a final Proclamation on those places that were still in rebellion but where he felt he did not have the constitutional authority to impose his will or his power as Commander in Chief, including parishes in Louisiana, as we know. Where there was a gray area, like the coastal areas, he had allowed emancipation to stand. That was the one day when there was a day of jubilee, because the emancipation affected the coastal areas immediately.

This whole notion of the language Lincoln used, the letters that he wrote publicly before he issued his preliminary Proclamation, the meetings he held in the White House with free African Americans at which he said very disobliging things with the newspaper stenographer intentionally invited to record the proceedings were all designed, as the *New York Tribune* wrote, to have a Proclamation that was completely based on military authority and not one out of "the bosom of philanthropy," to use a great quote from the *Tribune*.

I think Lincoln was not reluctant. I think he was petrified. He was petrified about losing border states, about losing Democratic support in the North, about maintaining the war, about losing the whole thing with the stroke of his pen. So I answer that he does not deserve less credit, but he certainly used enough cloudy language and political activity and press activity in the weeks leading up to it to keep this question raging for a long time.

WILLIAM ALEXANDER How do you think recent attention has really dealt with that issue in the latest historiography?

HAROLD HOLZER Well, it runs in phases. I certainly think Lincoln's reputation as a liberator is not what it was in the nineteenth century, among African Americans or whites where the entire story is known, but I think in many ways the arc has gone too far over to the other side. I am grateful and astonished and appreciative of what President Obama did when he put one of the surviving copies of the Proclamation from the edition that didn't sell in Philadelphia on view in the White House and brought civil rights veterans, including a 101-year-old woman named Mabel Harvey, into the room to see it. They were meeting in one cabinet room and they came into the Oval Office because he wanted to show them this frankly uninspiring piece of writing that begins with word "whereas." It was not calculated to stir souls. Mabel Harvey looked at it and said, "We've come a long way."

DAVID BLIGHT There is a book about to come out in a matter of days by Eric Foner, *The Fiery Trial*, about the historical origins of Lincoln's support of colonization, the plans and theories of removing African Americans from the United States. Not that it is necessarily corrective to what Harold just said, because Foner is an admirer of Lincoln as well, and of the Proclamation, but there is a story underneath this story about Lincoln's roots and background—the influence of Henry Clay and the Whig Party—and that shows us just how complicated the race question is when we talk about Lincoln.

JAMES McPHERSON I'd like to add something about Lincoln's background and the Emancipation Proclamation: Foner makes the point that Kentucky is the only state that has never ratified the Thirteenth, Fourteenth, or Fifteenth Amendments, and the congressional district where Lincoln was born in Kentucky voted against the Thirteenth Amendment. The congressional district that he represented in the 1840s in Illinois also voted against the Thirteenth Amendment.

So if you take into consideration Lincoln's background and the cultural influences where he grew up, it was all opposed to any of these developments. Lincoln transcended his background in a way that very few of the other people from that part of Kentucky or Illinois ever did.

HAROLD HOLZER We heard about Illinois this morning, from Professor Medford. Let us not forget that the only emotion Lincoln showed on election night in 1860 was after he learned he won his hometown by twenty votes. But after the Emancipation Proclamation, he lost his hometown in 1864.

WILLIAM ALEXANDER We have another question that tries to conflate the issue of slavery with that of race. Given the centrality of slavery in how Americans define race, why did the end of slavery not dismantle race as a defining characteristic of American people?

DAVID BLIGHT That is a great question and a complicated one. Well, all of these are complicated histories. Don't you hate it when historians just say it is complicated?

In many ways the end of slavery forced Americans to think in even greater racial terms or in a deeper kind of racialism. This goes back to what Ira Berlin explained earlier today: once the slaves were free and black people were no longer directly associated with bondage, well, then they had to have a new status, and this caused all kinds of crazy creativity in racial thinking.

If you really want to get to the heart of darkness about American racial thought, it was in the late nineteenth century. The end of slavery in many ways exacerbated or demanded a heightened awareness of who was white and who was black, and what was the legal status of these people who were supposed to be citizens now but were not quite full citizens.

In the midst of this enduring crazy American problem of federalism, did the states get to decide this or the federal government? Do the states still get to decide what the Fourteenth Amendment means, even though the federal government passed the Fourteenth Amendment and states ratified it? The end of slavery generated a heightened attention to what race and racism actually is.

JAMES HORTON From the standpoint of many people who were pro-slavery, the end of slavery meant the necessity for some other means of racial control. That helps to explain the significance of segregation because, among other things, it provided a kind of racial control.

You know, the racial segregation after slavery was different from slavery in terms of the separation of blacks and whites. Under slavery black people spent a lot of time in very close quarters with white people. It's true, they were their masters and their masters' family and friends, and so on; nevertheless, they spent time together. Segregation separated African Americans from white people. All of this happened in the late nineteenth and the early twentieth centuries. That situation still has a legacy today.

HAROLD HOLZER I always point to 1876 as the year of triple ironies. It is the year that the Ball statue was dedicated, with Frederick Douglass taking a sophisticated look at the Lincoln legacy, and he gave probably the greatest speech ever given about Abraham Lincoln. It was the year of the centennial of the Declaration of Independence and the re-evaluation of whether America had lived up to the "all men are created equal" promise. It was the year that the government bartered away federal occupation of the South and all hopes of a reconciliation that would embrace all people. There was a decade of possibility, but it ended abruptly.

DAVID BLIGHT If you want to understand how trapped Americans were in the racial ideology after slavery, look at the history of the Supreme Court, and what the justices appointed by Lincoln and Grant did with questions of race in the 1860s, 1870s, and 1880s. It is a sobering image of these brilliant justices, who nevertheless were trapped in a kind of racial ideology they could not transcend.

HAROLD HOLZER Chase died too soon.

DAVID BLIGHT Yes. Chase was about as liberal as anyone there.

HAROLD HOLZER And he was appointed specifically to safeguard freedom.

DWIGHT PITCAITHLEY One other event in 1876 was the demise of George Armstrong Custer at the Battle of Little Big Horn, which happened during the Philadelphia Centennial and encouraged the shift of federal energies from the South to the West.

JAMES McPHERSON In 1877 the Molly Maguires shifted attention to the labor question in the North.

JEAN FAGAN YELLIN You can see evidence of that on paper. Years ago I was reading the Quaker minute books, in beautiful handwriting, pages and pages about the relief the Quakers were sending to the South after the Civil War. They were paying for teachers and enlisting teachers and sending blankets and shoes. Then I literally turned the page, and saw that at their next meeting they were sending things to the Indians. I kept thinking a page was missing, but there was no page missing. They had just shifted their concern straight over.

DAVID BLIGHT Just wait until we get to the anniversary of 1876; now, there's a conference.

WILLIAM ALEXANDER Many in the audience have noted that this conference is about becoming American. Were there any discussions at the time of the Civil War of the contributions of blacks to American history as Africans? Was there any focus on that dimension? Not so much being absorbed into the United States but as Africans, the contributions of African history. We have heard how before, of course, Africa was demonized as a land without culture and so on. Were there any attempts to do the contrary?

HAROLD HOLZER You know, those who justified slavery spent so much time talking about how brilliant they had been in Christianizing Africans that unfortunately discussions of Africa often lead to discussions of colonization. So I do not think we see too much progress there.

DAVID BLIGHT The word "African" is still used in titling and labeling the African Methodist Episcopal Church. "African" was sometimes employed even in the names of some regiments. I do not know how many. But by the time of the Civil War there was an almost one hundred percent American born, black American population. There were very few

African-born African Americans, and what you really had here was a moment of unprecedented assertion, because of emancipation, of the American-ness of African Americans. You could argue—as many people have—that 1865, the year of the ratification of the Fourteenth Amendment, was the year when black Americans could identify with the United States far more than they would again for another century.

WILLIAM ALEXANDER But you do not see any attempt to perhaps refocus African history because of missionary activity and pluralism? Do you see any influence that that would have on the position of African Americans?

DAVID BLIGHT That did happen after the war. Henry McNeal Turner, for example, who was bishop of the AME Church, and others, even Alexander Crummell to a degree, became African-American thinkers, theologians in those two cases, who did begin to write African-American history. And they were not alone. There was a whole sort of sub-movement in black thought by the late nineteenth century of seeing African-American history, and therefore the emancipation of the slaves, in a kind of larger, biblical world history. In other words, the passage of Africans to America was just one piece of time immemorial and Africans were put in America for a greater purpose. There is a whole body of African-American theological thought that views emancipation in a biblical context. There you see the term "African" employed to a much greater degree, once again.

WILLIAM ALEXANDER This last question, a short one, brings us home. What were the motives of General Benjamin Butler before and after the contraband decision with regard to slaves, and what were the magnitude and the breadth of his position on slavery?

JAMES McPHERSON I will take a stab at that. Benjamin Butler had been a prominent Democrat in Massachusetts. He had actually supported Jefferson Davis in the Democratic Convention for the Presidential nomination in 1860. He had been appointed first as a Massachusetts militia major general and then by the Lincoln administration as a volunteer major general, because the Lincoln administration was eager to bring Democrats into the coalition to prosecute the war. So that is how he got his position. When he first entered Maryland during the occupation of Baltimore in May of 1861, he had offered to put down a slave insurrection if it happened there.

So one would not predict that he would turn into a radical Republican. But at some point he must have made the decision that that was where the future was going. He had a somewhat cynical attitude, and when a Confederate colonel came to ask him to return these fugitive slaves owned by the Confederates, one of them owned by the colonel himself, I think, Butler said that Virginia no longer belonged to the Union, so the Fugitive Slave Act did not apply anymore to Virginia. He then came up with the idea of the contraband in the war, and from then on it was a road to the left for Benjamin Butler until he became one of the most prominent radical Republicans. He was beginning to see which way the wind was blowing on this question.

Conference Participants

JAMES OLIVER HORTON, Conference Chair, is the Benjamin Banneker Professor Emeritus of American Studies and History at George Washington University. He taught at the university for more than thirty years before retiring in 2008. He is also Historian Emeritus at the National Museum of American History at the Smithsonian Institution, and during spring semesters, Visiting Professor of American Studies at the University of Hawaii. He earned a Ph.D. in history from Brandeis University in 1973 and taught at the University of Michigan from 1973 until 1977 when he moved to George Washington University.

He was Senior Fulbright Professor of American Studies at the University of Munich, in Germany in 1988–89 and the John Adams Distinguished Fulbright Chair in American History at the University of Leiden in the Netherlands in the fall of 2003. He has lectured throughout Europe and in Thailand and Japan. In 1991 he assisted the German government in developing American Studies programs in the former East Germany.

Professor Horton was appointed to the National Park System Advisory Board in 1993. In 1994–95 he served as Senior Advisor on Historical Interpretation and Public Education for the Director of the National Park Service.

IRA BERLIN is Distinguished University Professor in the Department of History at the University of Maryland, where he served as Dean of Undergraduates and Dean of the College of Arts and Humanities. He attended New York public schools and the University of Wisconsin, where in 1970 he received a doctorate in history with high honors. In 1990, he was appointed Distinguished Teacher-Scholar, and in 1991 the Maryland Association for Higher Education named him the state's Outstanding Educator.

Ira Berlin has written extensively on American history in the eighteenth and nineteenth centuries, particularly on Southern and African-American life. His first book, *Slaves Without Masters: The Free Negro in the Antebellum South* (1975) won the Best First Book Prize awarded by the National Historical Society. Berlin is the founder of the Freedmen and Southern Society Project, which he directed until 1991. The project's multi-volume *Freedom: A Documentary History of Emancipation* (1982, 1985, 1990, 1993) has twice been awarded the Thomas Jefferson Prize of the Society for History in the Federal Government as well as the J. Franklin Jameson Prize of the American Historical Association for outstanding editorial achievement, and the Abraham Lincoln Prize for excellence in Civil War studies from the Lincoln and Soldiers Institute of Gettysburg College.

His articles and reviews have appeared in the *New York Times, Washington Post, Philadelphia Inquirer, The Nation, American Historical Review, Journal of American History, Journal of Social History, Journal of Negro History, William and Mary Quarterly*, and other popular and scholarly periodicals.

DAVID W. BLIGHT is Class of 1954 Professor of American History at Yale University, having joined that faculty in January 2003. He previously taught at Amherst College for thirteen years. As of June 2004, he is Director of the Gilder Lehrman Center for the Study of Slavery, Resistance, and Abolition at Yale. During the 2006–07 academic year he was a fellow at the Dorothy and Lewis B. Cullman Center for Writers and Scholars, New York Public Library.

Blight is a frequent book reviewer for *Washington Post Book World, Los Angeles Times*, and *Boston Globe* and is one of the authors of the bestselling American history textbook for the college level, *A People and a Nation*. His book, *Race and Reunion: The*

Civil War in American Memory (Harvard University Press, 2001), received eight awards, including the Bancroft Prize, the Abraham Lincoln Prize, the Frederick Douglass Prize, and four awards from the Organization of American Historians. Blight's most recent book, *A Slave No More: Two Men Who Escaped to Freedom, Including Their Narratives of Emancipation*, was published by Harcourt in 2007.

SPENCER CREW has worked in public history institutions for more than twenty-five years. He served as president of the National Underground Railroad Freedom Center for six years and worked at the National Museum of American History, Smithsonian Institution for twenty years. Nine of those years he served as the director of NMAH. At each of those institutions he sought to make history accessible to the public through innovative and inclusive exhibitions and public programs.

HAROLD HOLZER, Senior Vice President for External Affairs at the Metropolitan Museum of Art, serves also as co-chairman of the U.S. Abraham Lincoln Bicentennial Commission. He is the author, co-author, or editor of thirty-five books on Lincoln and the Civil War era. His latest books are: *Lincoln President-Elect: Abraham Lincoln and the Great Secession Winter 1860–1861* (2008), which won the Barondess/Lincoln Award and the Award of Achievement of the Lincoln Group of New York; *The Lincoln Anthology* (2009), a Library of America collection featuring great writers on the subject of Abraham Lincoln; *In Lincoln's Hand* (2009), featuring Lincoln's original manuscripts with commentary by distinguished Americans; and *Lincoln and New York* (2009), the catalogue of a New York Historical Society exhibition for which he served as chief historian.

Holzer has also written many articles and chapters over the past thirty-five years in both scholarly and popular publications, and he has received research and writing awards, most recently the National Endowment Medal in 2008. A former journalist and political and government press secretary (for Bella Abzug and Mario Cuomo), Holzer has served as an executive at the Metropolitan Museum of Art since 1992. He and his wife,

Edith, who live in Rye, New York, have two grown daughters and a grandson.

BRUCE LEVINE is the J. G. Randall Distinguished Professor of History at the University of Illinois, Urbana-Champaign. He has published three books on the era of the Civil War. The first, *The Spirit of 1848: German Immigrants, Labor Conflict, and the Coming of Civil War* (University of Illinois, 1992), examines immigrants' reactions to slavery and the sectional conflict in America. The second, *Half Slave and Half Free: The Roots of Civil War* (Hill & Wang, 1992; revised 2005), explores the social, economic, and political causes of the war. The third, *Confederate Emancipation: Southern Plans to Free and Arm Slaves during the Civil War* (Oxford, 2005), analyzes the Confederacy's desperate, last-minute attempt to win the war by enlisting and emancipating its own slaves.

   Confederate Emancipation received the Peter Seaborg Award for Civil War Scholarship and was named by the *Washington Post* as one of the year's ten best books. Levine's next book will describe the destruction of slavery and the South's slave-based society during the Civil War.

JAMES M. MCPHERSON was born in North Dakota and grew up in Minnesota, where he graduated from Gustavus Adolphus College in 1958. In 1963 he received a Ph.D. from Johns Hopkins University. From 1962 until retirement in 2004, he taught American history at Princeton University, where he is now the George Henry Davis `86 Professor of American History Emeritus. He is the author of fifteen books and editor of another ten books, most of them on the era of the American Civil War and Reconstruction.

   His books have won several prizes, including the Pulitzer Prize (1989) for *Battle Cry of Freedom: The Civil War Era*; a Lincoln Prize (1998) for *For Cause and Comrades: Why Men Fought in the Civil War*; and a second Lincoln Prize (2009) for *Tried by War: Abraham Lincoln as Commander in Chief.* He has received a number of other awards, including the Pritzker Prize for lifetime achievement in military writing. He is now working on a book about the navies in the Civil War.

EDNA GREENE MEDFORD is Professor and Chairperson of the Department of History at Howard University. Specializing in nineteenth century African-American history, Professor Medford teaches and lectures widely to scholarly and community-based groups and has presented to international audiences on topics that range from Alexis de Tocqueville to community-building among American free blacks in Civil War-era Canada. She has served as the Director for History of New York's African Burial Ground Project since 1996, and edited the project's history report. She has published more than a dozen articles and book chapters on African Americans, especially during the era of the Civil War. Her publications include *The Emancipation Proclamation: Three Views* (with co-authors Harold Holzer and Frank Williams).

She has appeared on several segments of the History Channel's "Civil War Journal" and on a number of C-SPAN programs. She is the 2006 recipient of the "Outstanding Graduate Faculty of the Year Award" for the Graduate School of Arts and Sciences (awarded by the Graduate Student Assembly). Her research awards include a National Endowment for the Humanities grant to complete a study of community-building across international boundaries among nineteenth century African Americans and African Canadians.

CASSANDRA NEWBY-ALEXANDER has always tried to integrate teaching, research, and public service in the greater service of learning. She has focused much of her research and writing on the history of African Americans in Virginia. Her publications have appeared in edited books and major bio-graphical series, such as the *Dictionary of Virginia Biography*. Her next project will examine the Underground Railroad in Virginia.

She has been a pioneer in the application of technology to teaching history, creating the digitally-based history project, "Race, Time, and Place: African Americans in Tidewater Virginia" in 1999. In addition to her scholarly activities, she is civically active, serving on numerous community boards (including the Virginia Foundation for the Humanities, the Historical Commission of the Supreme Court of Virginia, and the Norfolk Sister City Association), making historical presentations to local schools and community organizations, and appearing on local television and radio programming about the United States, Hampton Roads, and local African-American history.

DWIGHT T. PITCAITHLEY received his Ph.D. from Texas Tech University in 1976 and has developed a long career in public history ever since. Before becoming a college professor, he worked for the National Park Service for over thirty years as historian for the Southwest Region based in Sante Fe, New Mexico, in the North Atlantic Region based in Boston, and in Washington, D.C. From 1995 to 2005, he served as Chief Historian for the National Park Service.

Throughout his career, Professor Pitcaithley has been involved with the National Council on Public History and served on editorial boards for *Public Historian* and *Journal of American History*. He is currently Professor of History at New Mexico State University and serves on the Board of Directors for the New Mexico Humanities Council.

JEAN FAGAN YELLIN was born into a radical Midwestern newspaper family and earned her graduate degrees at the University of Illinois. A Distinguished Professor Emerita at Pace University, New York, she has edited *Uncle Tom's Cabin* and other classic American texts and is best known for her work on the fugitive slave author and activist Harriet Jacobs. She published the definitive edition of Jacobs' *Incidents in the Life of a Slave Girl*, establishing the book as autobiography and Jacobs as its author; wrote the biography *Harriet Jacobs: A Life* (2004); and edited the two-volume *Harriet Jacobs Family Papers* (2008). Also the author of *Women and Sisters* and *The Intricate Knot*, she is a mother, a grandmother, and a great-grandmother. With her husband, she divides her time between New York City and Sarasota, Florida.

Further Reading

Source material

Brown, Peter A., ed. *Take Sides with the Truth: The Postwar Letters of John Singleton Mosby*. Lexington: University Press of Kentucky, 2007.

Brown, William Wells. *The Narrative of William W. Brown, a Fugitive Slave*. 1848. Reprint, Reading, MA: Addison-Wesley, 1969.

Douglass, Frederick. *Narrative of the Life of Frederick Douglass*. 1845.

Gould IV, William B. *Diary of a Contraband: The Civil War Passage of a Black Sailor*. Stanford, CA: Stanford University Press, 2002.

Hayes, John D., ed. *Samuel Francis Du Pont: A Selection from His Civil War Letters*. 3 volumes. Ithaca, NY: Cornell University Press, 1969.

Northup, Solomon. *Twelve Years a Slave: Narrative of Solomon Northup, a citizen of New-York, kidnapped in Washington city in 1841, and rescued in 1853, from a cotton plantation near the Red River in Louisiana*. 1853.

Official Records of the Union and Confederate Navies in the War of the Rebellion. 30 volumes. Washington, DC: Government Printing Office, 1894–1922.

Proceedings of the Virginia Secession Convention. Richmond, VA: University of Richmond. http://collections.richmond.edu/secession.

Rutherford, Mildred Lewis. *The South Must Have Her Rightful Place in History*. Athens, GA: 1923.

Rutherford, Mildred Lewis. *The Truths of History: A Fair, Unbiased, Impartial, Unprejudiced, and Conscientious Study of History.* Athens, GA: 1920.

Still, William. *The Underground Railroad.* Philadelphia: Porter & Coates, 1872.

Symonds, Craig L., ed. *Charleston Blockade: The Journals of John B. Marchand, U.S. Navy, 1861–62.* Newport, RI: Naval War College Press, 1976.

Washington, Booker T. *Up From Slavery.* New York: Doubleday, Page, 1901.

Yellin, Jean Fagan. *Harriet Jacobs: A Life.* New York: Basic Civitas Books, 2004.

ABRAHAM LINCOLN

Basler, Roy P., ed. *The Collected Works of Abraham Lincoln.* 9 volumes. New Brunswick, NJ: Rutgers University Press, 1953–55.

Cox, Lawanda F. *Lincoln and Black Freedom: A Study in Presidential Leadership.* Columbia: University of South Carolina Press, 1994.

Escott, Paul D. *"What Shall We Do with the Negro?" Lincoln, White Racism, and Civil War America.* Charlottesville: University of Virginia Press, 2009.

Foner, Eric. *The Fiery Trial: Abraham Lincoln and American Slavery.* New York: Norton, 2010.

Foner, Eric. *Our Lincoln: New Perspectives on Lincoln and His World.* New York: Norton, 2008.

Gienapp, William. *Abraham Lincoln and Civil War America.* New York: Oxford University Press, 2002.

Guelzo, Allen C. *Lincoln's Emancipation Proclamation: The End of Slavery in America.* New York: Simon & Schuster, 2004.

Holzer, Harold, Gabor S. Boritt, and Mark E. Neely, Jr. *The Lincoln Image: Abraham Lincoln and the Popular Print.* Urbana: University of Illinois Press, 2001.

Jaffa, Harry V. *A New Birth of Freedom: Abraham Lincoln and the Coming of the Civil War.* Lanham, MD: Rowman & Littlefield, 2000.

Jones, Howard. *Abraham Lincoln and a New Birth of Freedom: The Union and Slavery in the Diplomacy of the Civil War.* Lincoln: University of Nebraska Press, 2002.

Klingaman, William K. *Abraham Lincoln and the Road to Emancipation.* New York: Viking, 2001.

Peterson, Merrill D. *Lincoln in American Memory.* New York: Oxford University Press, 1994.

Rubenstein, Harry R. and the National Museum of American History. *Abraham Lincoln: An Extraordinary Life.* Washington, DC: Smithsonian Institution Press, 2009.

AFRICAN-AMERICAN SOLDIERS

Berlin, Ira, et al., ed. *Freedom's Soldiers: The Black Military Experience in the Civil War.* New York: Cambridge University Press, 1998.

Cornish, Dudley Taylor. *The Sable Arm: Negro Troops in the Union Army, 1861–1865.* New York: Longmans Green, 1956.

Glatthaar, Joseph T. *The Civil War's Black Soldiers.* Conshohocken, PA: Eastern National Park and Monument Association, 1996.

Glatthaar, Joseph T. *Forged in Battle: The Civil War Alliance of Black Soldiers and White Officers.* New York: Free Press, 1990.

Longacre, Edward G. *A Regiment of Slaves: The 4th United States Colored Infantry, 1863–1866.* Mechanicsburg, PA: Stackpole Books, 2003.

BLACK CONFEDERATES

Brewer, James H. *The Confederate Negro: Virginia's Craftsmen and Military Laborers, 1861–1865.* Durham, NC: Duke University Press, 1969.

Jordan, Jr., Ervin L. *Black Confederates and Afro-Yankees in Civil War Virginia.* Charlottesville: University of Virginia Press, 1995.

Levine, Bruce. *Confederate Emancipation: Southern Plans to Free and Arm Slaves during the Civil War.* New York: Oxford University Press, 2005.

SLAVERY AND EMANCIPATION

Ash, Steven V. *Black Experience in the Civil War South.* Santa Barbara, CA: Prager, 2010.

Berlin, Ira et al., ed. *Free at Last: A Documentary History of Slavery, Freedom, and the Civil War.* New York: The New Press, 1992.

Blight, David. *A Slave No More: Two Men Who Escaped to Freedom, Including Their Own Narratives of Emancipation.* New York: Harcourt, 2007.

Carson, Clayborne, Emma J. Lapsansky-Werner, and Gary B. Nash. *African American Lives: The Struggle for Freedom*. Combined volume. New York: Pearson Longman, 2004.

Hahn, Steven. *A Nation Under Our Feet: Black Political Struggles in the Rural South from Slavery to the Great Migration*. Cambridge, MA: Harvard University Press, 2003.

Harrold, Stanley. *Border War: Fighting over Slavery before the Civil War*. Chapel Hill: University of North Carolina Press, 2010.

Holzer, Harold, Edna Greene Medford, and Frank J. Williams. *The Emancipation Proclamation: Three Views (social, political, iconographic)*. Baton Rouge: Louisiana State University Press, 2006.

Manning, Chandra. *What This Cruel War Was Over: Soldiers, Slavery, and the Civil War*. New York: Vintage Books, 2008.

Robinson, Armstead L. *Bitter Fruits of Bondage: The Demise of Slavery and the Collapse of the Confederacy, 1861–1865*. Charlottesville: University of Virginia Press, 2005.

THE CIVIL WAR IN AMERICAN MEMORY

Ayers, Edward L. *What Caused the Civil War? Reflections on the South and Southern History*. New York: Norton, 2005.

Blight, David. *Race and Reunion: The Civil War in American Memory*. Cambridge, MA: Belknap Press, 2001.

Horton, James Oliver and Lois E. Horton, ed. *Slavery and Public History: The Tough Stuff of American Memory*. New York: New Press, 2006.

SECESSION AND CIVIL WAR

Ayers, Edward L., Gary W. Gallagher, and Andrew J. Torget, ed. *Crucible of the Civil War: Virginia from Secession to Commemoration*. Charlottesville: University of Virginia Press, 2006.

Catton, Bruce. *Civil War Trilogy: Mr Lincoln's Army, Glory Road, and A Stillness at Appomattox*. London: Phoenix Press, 2001.

Dew, Charles. *Apostles of Disunion: Southern Secession Commissioners and the Causes of the Civil War*. Charlottesville: University of Virginia Press, 2002.

Foote, Shelby. *The Civil War: A Narrative*. Volume 1: *Fort Sumter to Perryville*. New York: Random House, 1958. Volume 2: *Fredericksburg to Meridian*. New York: Random House, 1963. Volume 3: *Red River to Appomattox*. New York: Random House, 1974.

Freehling, William. *The Road to Disunion.* Volume 1: *Secessionists at Bay, 1776–1854.* New York: Oxford University Press, 1991. Volume 2: *Secessionists Triumphant, 1854–1861.* New York: Oxford University Press, 2007.

Holzer, Harold and Craig L. Symonds, ed. *The New York Times Complete Civil War 1861–1865.* New York: Black Dog and Leventhal, 2010.

Lankford, Nelson D. *Cry Havoc! The Crooked Road to Civil War, 1861.* New York: Viking, 2007.

McCurry, Stephanie. *Confederate Reckoning: Power and Politics in the Civil War South.* Cambridge, MA: Harvard University Press, 2010.

McPherson, James M. *Battle Cry of Freedom: The Civil War Era.* New York: Oxford University Press, 1988.

McPherson, James M., ed. *Encyclopedia of Civil War Biographies.* 3 volumes. Armonk, NY: Sharpe Reference, 2000.

THE UNDERGROUND RAILROAD

Bordewich, Fergus M. *Bound for Canaan: The Underground Railroad and the War for the Soul of America.* New York: Amistad, 2005.

Clinton, Catharine. *Harriet Tubman: The Road to Freedom.* New York: Little, Brown, 2005.

INDEX

SIGNATURE CONFERENCE SERIES

2009   AMERICA ON THE EVE OF THE CIVIL WAR
        University of Richmond
        April 29, 2009

2010   RACE, SLAVERY AND THE CIVIL WAR
        Norfolk State University
        September 24, 2010

2011   MILITARY STRATEGY IN THE AMERICAN
        CIVIL WAR
        Virginia Tech
        May 21, 2011

2012   LEADERSHIP AND GENERALSHIP IN THE
        CIVIL WAR
        Virginia Military Institute
        March 22, 2012

2013   THE HOME FRONT IN THE CIVIL WAR
        College of William and Mary

2014   THE AMERICAN CIVIL WAR IN A GLOBAL
        CONTEXT
        George Mason University

2015   MEMORY OF THE CIVIL WAR
        University of Virginia

Tentative schedule. The Signature Conference series is a project of the Virginia
Sesquicentennial of the American Civil War Commission.